The Cognitive Demands of Writing

The Cognitive Demands of Writing

Processing Capacity and Working Memory in Text Production

Edited by
Mark Torrance
Gaynor C. Jeffery

AMSTERDAM UNIVERSITY PRESS

Studies in Writing

General editors: Gert Rijlaarsdam and Eric Espéret

Effective Teaching and Learning of Writing
Current Trends in Research
edited by Gert Rijlaarsdam, Huub van den Bergh and Michel Couzijn

Theories, Models and Methodology in Writing Research
edited by Gert Rijlaarsdam, Huub van den Bergh and Michel Couzijn

According to the Publication Manual of the American Psychological Association (4th Edition), one should refer to this work as to chapters in a volume series: [Authors of the chapter] [1998] [Title of the chapter]. In G. Rijlaarsdam & E. Esperet (Series Eds.) & M. Torrance & G. Jefferey (Vol. Eds.) *Studies in Writing: Vol. 3. The Cognitive Demands of Writing*. [pages]. Amsterdam: Amsterdam University Press.

Cover design: NAP-ontwerpers, Amsterdam
Typesetting: BEELDVORM, Leidschendam

ISBN 90 5356 308 3

© Amsterdam University Press, Amsterdam, 1999

Preface

To us, this third volume of Studies in Writing is again an excellent example how fruitful international co-operation in research can be. Because of the specialisation of research, it is getting more and more difficult to get an overall picture of a certain research topic. In our opinion, Mark Torrance and Gaynor Jeffery as guest editors invited a very strong group of authors and guided them to publish an excellent book on a often neglected but very basic field in the domain of writing.

Although a cliché, stating that writing is a complex activity that places considerable demands on writers' cognitive resources, is nevertheless a fact. This volume presents original theory and research exploring the ways in which the sub-components of the writing process (generating and organising content, producing grammatical sentences and so forth) differ in their cognitive demands and examines how writers manage these when producing text. We recommend the book to writing researchers, to cognitive psychologists and psycholinguists with an interest in attention and working memory in language production, and to any reader who seeks an understanding of the cognitive mechanisms that lie behind the writing process.

Gert Rijlaarsdam
University of Amsterdam

Eric Espéret
University of Poitiers

Contents

Writing processes and cognitive demands

Mark Torrance
Institute of Behavioural Sciences, University of Derby, UK
Gaynor Jeffery
Department of Psychology, University of Southampton, UK

1 INTRODUCTION

The following is a writer describing the experience of converting ideas into text:

The initial gurgitation of material builds up a high pressure of nervous excitement leading to such physical symptoms as redness in the face, headache, inability to sit down, lapses of concentration and extreme short temper, especially on interruption. Ordering the material presents agonising problems of rethinking [....] problems of sequencing often lead to inability of write down a coherent sentence. The final process well nigh unendurable (Lowenthal and Wason, 1977, p 781)

Writing, for many people and for most kinds of writing task, appears to demand considerable cognitive resources. So much so, in fact, that there is a constant risk that the whole writing system will become overloaded to the detriment, at best, of the quality of the text that is being produced and, at worst, to normal social functioning (or so appeared to be the case with the unfortunate writer quoted above). Experienced writers' self reports typically describe the need for concentrated and uninterrupted effort if writing is to be successful (e.g., Plimpton, 1965; Cohen, 1977; Hartley and Knapper, 1984). Some writers' working habits - writing only in the early morning, late at night, in a shed at the bottom of the garden - seem motivated by their perception that the process of writing requires exceptional levels of attention.

Most existing cognitive theories of the writing process paint a similar picture. According to these theories, text production involves the complex interplay of several different sub-processes or functions (content generation, content organisation, lexicalisation, transcription, reading) and for this reason is likely to be resource demanding (McCutchen, 1996; Hayes, 1996). Some researchers have gone so far as to argue that expertise in writing breaks the rules that apply to expert performance in other domains. Experts in most fields appear to be able to perform tasks that lie within their domain of expertise with relative ease and with little conscious access to their mental processes. By contrast, expert writers appear to agonise more over their text, engaging in substantially more explicit planning and problem solving, than do novices (Scardamalia and Bereiter, 1991).

This is not the whole picture, however. Although it is generally assumed that most writers find writing laborious, writing folklore is replete with stories of a friend of a colleague who is able to sit down and effortlessly write out full and well formed papers in a single draft without editing. Even if these stories are apocryphal it is certainly the case that some writing tasks can be performed by some or most writers with relatively little effort. Writing letters to friends, comments on a student's essay, directions to your house and so forth, all appear to involve less effort than writing the opening paragraphs of a book chapter. There is also some evidence that more substantial writing tasks, particularly in contexts where the genre is familiar, may be possible with substantially less elaborate processing than is indicated by existing cognitive models (Schilperoord, 1996; Schumacher et al, 1989; Torrance, 1996a). Direct measures of cognitive effort suggest that writers with greater knowledge of the subject matter of their text place less demand on cognitive resources than less knowledgeable writers (Kellogg, this volume). Conversely, it is possible to make what should be an undemanding writing task demanding by, for example, requiring that writers use only upper-case letters (Bourdin and Fayol, 1994) or that they attempt to remember a set of numbers while they are writing (Jeffery and Underwood, 1995; Kellogg, this volume).

An adequate theory of the ways in which text production makes use of writers' limited cognitive resources needs, therefore, to go beyond asking "why is writing difficult?". It must account for the effects of factors associated with the writer's expertise and content knowledge and with the nature of the writing task. It will also need to take into account the complexity of text production. What is sometimes loosely referred to as "the writing process" is composed of a number of different activities each associated with different cognitive processes and, consequently, with different cognitive demands. The picture is further complicated by considering the nature of the cognitive resources themselves. It seems likely that not all cognitive capacity is available to all cognitive processes but that specific resources are dedicated to processing specific kinds of representation. If this is the case then we need to know not just whether a writing sub-process demands cognitive resources, but what kinds of resources it requires and whether it is likely to have to compete for these with other processes.

To be able to predict the extent to which a writer is loading her cognitive capacity at a particular point in time (which seems an appropriate goal for a cognitive capacity theory of writing) we therefore need to have, at least, (a) an understanding of the individual and task variables that affect text production, (b) an adequate theory of how people process information to generate text, and (c) an understanding of the cognitive architecture within which these processes run. Each of these is, of course, dependent, to a greater or lesser extent, on the others. An account of relevant writer and task variables and their effects on processing demands - perhaps the most educationally pertinent end product of research in this area - is not possible outside of a theory of the cognitive components of the writing process and how these function. Accounts of what processing resources are available and how these are deployed are, in turn, necessary to constrain how the writing process is theorised: however comprehensive and cohesive a model might otherwise appear, if in order to run successfully it requires more cognitive resources than existing evidence suggests are likely to be available then the theory needs to be modified.

There is considerable debate about the nature both of the writing process and of the mind's cognitive resources. Theory in both these areas is, however, sufficiently rich to form the basis for an exploration of the ways in which writing processes and cognitive resources interact. From the perspective of the small band of cognitive psychologists whose research has focussed on writing this is a particularly satisfying project. Whereas research on text comprehension has been at the heart of developing general theories of cognitive capacity, text production research has in the past failed to impact on these debates or, come to that, on many of the debates that interest mainstream cognitive psychologists. This is now changing, as is evidenced by the chapters that follow. They present a wealth of new research focussed on interpreting writing behaviour in the context of existing theories of attention, working memory and processing resources. This research provides a richer understanding of the psychology of writing than has previously been available. Additionally, and excitingly, by bringing existing theories of human cognitive capacity to bear on a cognitive function that has not previously been studied in this context, the chapters that follow provide a new critique of these theories and suggest ways in which they might be developed.

In the remainder of this introductory chapter, we will first briefly describe some of the parameters that delineate current debate over the processing and short-term storage of information during the performance of complex cognitive tasks, a debate that re-emerges in the chapters that follow. Next we provide a (again very brief) sketch of existing cognitive accounts of the writing process. We then look at how these processes might be shaped by having to operate within a limited cognitive capacity. Finally, we give a short overview of the rest of the book.

2 PROCESSING CAPACITY AND WORKING MEMORY

Everyday observation suggests that it is not possible to concentrate on a large number of things at once: long complex arguments require re-reading, telephone numbers of over ten digits need to be written down, telephoning rail enquiries and typing a chapter need to be performed sequentially rather than simultaneously. Humans, despite being able to permanently store very large amounts of information, are only able to work on a very small amount of this information at any one time. Cognitive capacity theories seek to explain exactly how much information, and of what kind, can be held active and processed.

Comprehensive overviews of different ways in which capacity has been theorised are available elsewhere (e.g., Richardson, 1996) and are usefully discussed in some detail, and with an emphasis on resource use in writing, by Lea and Levy in this volume. Despite considerable bodies of research in this area, there is relatively little agreement about how capacity should be theorised. Broadly, debate centres around four issues.

Single vs. multiple resources. Cognitive capacity may be shared by all processes and kinds of information or may be partitioned in some way. At its simplest, cognitive capacity might be conceptualised in exactly the same way as computer users conceptualise random access memory: there is a certain amount of capacity within which programs can run, and when this is exceeded there is either a general slowing of performance or one or more programs will crash. There are at least two alternatives to this position, both of which seek to explain why some combinations of cognitive tasks can be performed simultaneously more easily and with more success than other combinations (holding a conversation while driving, for example, is easier than holding a conversation whilst doing a crossword puzzle). One possibility is that some of the resources are dedicated to specific kinds of process or information. Thus verbal tasks, for example, draw on verbal resources leaving other resources more or less in tact. Alternatively, it may be that specific processes are informationally encapsulated (Fodor, 1983; Stanovich, 1990) and thus cannot be interfered with once they start to run, regardless of the nature of other current processes.

Resource vs. structure. Limits on the amount of information that can be held active at any one time can be theorised in terms of general limits of processing resources (a trading metaphor) or in terms of mental structures (a spatial metaphor). Resource theories talk in general terms of the quantity of cognitive resources available to a particular process. Structural theories specify control mechanisms that govern the flow of information into short-term storage where it can be attended to and worked upon.

Storage vs. processing. There is a distinction between the use of processing capacity to store the information that is needed for currently active processes and the demands of the processing itself. Depending on how cognitive resources are structured, it is possible that both processing and storage will compete for the same resources. If this is the case then experience in performing a task, with resulting automaticity of processing is likely to be rewarded by increased short-term storage capacity. Thus experienced readers, for example, are able to hold more words within short term memory while they are reading than are less experienced readers (Daneman and Carpenter, 1980). Ransdell and Levy's chapter discusses this issue in some detail and describes memory span tasks specifically targeted at measuring the storage capacity available to writers while they are writing.

Short term vs. long term storage. Finally, there are two ways in which a concept or process can be available for immediate processing. It may be that for a concept or process to be readily available it must make use of processing capacity. Alternatively, it may be that some concepts and processes, if they are well learned, are always immediately available for processing (Logie, 1996; Ericsson and Kintsch, 1995). According to this account it is not necessary to keep all the information associated with concepts or processes currently in use active. All that is held active is a label or pointer that provides a very fast link to the required information which remains in permanent storage.

Therefore, although it would appear that there is a definite underlying phenomenon to be explained - people cannot perform more than one or two cognitive operations at any one time - there is a wide range of frameworks within which this phenomenon can be theorised. This makes it difficult to find a single term for what we are talking about (both *cognitive resources* and *cognitive capacity* which we have used thus far in this chapter suggest particular theoretical positions). *Working memory* has gained popularity as a catch all title for these processes (Richardson, 1996). Confusingly, however, working memory also is the name given to a specific model of short-term storage and processing developed by Baddeley and co-workers (e.g., Baddeley and Hitch, 1974; Baddeley, 1990). This model is the basis for the research reported in the chapters by Kellogg, and by Levy and Marek in this volume. It has also played an important role in previous discussions of the processing demands of writing (Hayes, 1996; Jeffery and Underwood, 1995; Kellogg, 1996; Ransdell and Levy, 1996).

Baddeley's conception of working memory, which is summarised by Levy and Marek (Chapter 3) and critically discussed by Lea and Levy (Chapter 5), involves multiple resources with separate storage capacity dedicated to phonological and to visuo-spatial representations. It is a structural model in that it has three distinct components - two slave systems and a central executive - each with its own characteristics. There is debate over the extent to which components of the model are dedicated to storage or processing. In recent conceptualisations, the central executive does not store information but is rather a processing or even purely attentional device. The two slave systems, however, are still considered to have some storage function (Baddeley, 1993; Richardson, 1996). Finally, original conceptions of working memory saw it as an entirely short-term storage device. Logie (1996), however, has suggested that it might be better understood as a workspace that has some storage capabilities but which also allows rapid access to permanently stored information. Baddeley's model has been, until recently, almost exclusively the domain of European researchers where it has dominated as an account of short-term storage.

3   THE WRITING PROCESS

The process of producing text is typically thought of as involving three activities: Writers *plan* what they are going to say and how they are going to say it, they *translate* these plans into sentences, and they *review* what they have written to ensure that it says what they want it to say. Although there is a necessary progression from plan to text to review, which is evident in most writers' behaviour (e.g., Kellogg, 1987), writers appear to be able to move freely between these activities (Hayes and Flower, 1980). Planning, for example, tends to appear not only at the start of the production of a document but will also interrupt translation and, less frequently, revision. Its occurrence is related to the structure of the text, with more planning occurring at paragraph boundaries than at sentence boundaries or within sentences (Schilperoord, 1996; Dansac and Alamargot, 1998). The moment by moment transition from one activity to another appears to form patterns that are, to some extent, stable within individuals (Levy and Ransdell, 1995) and, more broadly, different writing strategies can be identified in terms of variation among writers in the prevalence of each writing activity at different points in the writing process (van Waes, 1992; Torrance, Thomas and Robinson, in press).

Less is known about the cognitive processes that make planning, translation and review possible. Hayes and Flower (1980), who were probably the first researchers to take seriously the possibility of a comprehensive cognitive theory of the writing process, suggested some ways in which each activity might be modelled. Their account was set loosely within the framework of Newell and Simon's theory of human problem solving (Newell and Simon, 1972) and thus represented writing processes in terms of broad production rules mapping the writer's intention onto actions. This approach has not been adopted in recent research, although production rules that are much closer to the text structure may be a useful way of accounting for inter-writer differences (see, for example, van Wijk, 1998). However, their account has served to draw attention to the multiple constraints that compete for writers' attention as they produce text (Flower and Hayes, 1980a; McCutchen, 1996). Deciding which word to use next, for example, is constrained at least (a) by the syntax of the sentence to which it contributes, (b) by the writer's intended message, (c) by the need to maintain coherence across sentences, (d) by whether a direct or anaphoric reference is appropriate, (e) by the perceived register of the discourse community to whom the text is directed, and (f) by the need to avoid overusing the same word. The processing associated with managing each of these constraints is likely to be complex and to make some demand on processing resources.

It is not however particularly clear where to draw the boundaries between the different functions that writing sub-processes perform. Flower and Hayes, for example, make considerable play of the need for writers to explicitly process what they describe as the "rhetorical problem", an amalgam of knowledge about the needs of the intended audience and the writer's intended message (Flower and Hayes, 1980b). It seems possible, however, that the function played by the setting of high level goals in Hayes and Flower's model might be achieved either by importing ready-made rhetorical schemas into the writing process (Schilperoord, 1996; Schilperoord and Sanders, 1998; Torrance, 1996b) or through low level, probabilistic search of semantic memory (Galbraith, 1998; Torrance, Thomas and Robinson, 1996).

4   CAPACITY CONSTRAINTS AND THE WRITING PROCESS

Whatever the details of the underlying operations, it is generally accepted that writing is sufficiently complex to risk overloading cognitive resources (e.g., Kellogg, 1988). The thrust of Michel Fayol's chapter in this volume is that even processes that might be assumed to be more or less automatic in competent writers (maintaining noun-verb agreement or legible handwriting, for example) appear to involve some processing costs. Not only might different sub-processes compete for processing resources, but each process will also require active storage of varying amounts of information. Bereiter and Scardamalia estimated that the absolute minimum requirement for maintaining local coherence is that two chunks of information are held active (Bereiter and Scardamalia, 1987, p151).

There are at least three ways in which writers' cognitive processes are adapted to utilise available capacity best. First, the writing process, as described by Hayes and Flower, is probably relatively rarely implemented in full. Hayes and Flower (1980; Flower and Hayes, 1980a) deliberately set out to model their conception of what constitutes competent writing performance. Accordingly, they presented a normative account of writing that centres around goal setting and problem solving activities (an emphasis that is tempered in Hayes' recent revisiting of the earlier theory [Hayes, 1996]). It appears, however, that a large number of writers, and particularly novice writers, do not engage in these activities. Bereiter and Scardamalia (1987, pp6-12; Bereiter, Burtis and Scardamalia, 1988) have suggested a simplified model that allows for text production based on processes that do not require explicit goal setting or problem solving. They argue that this "knowledge-telling" approach is less developmentally advanced. It provides a means of writing that places less demand on processing and storage resources than does the full blown problem solving approach, which Bereiter and Scardamalia describe as knowledge transforming. For novice writers who have less automaticity in, for example, syntactic planning or spelling, knowledge telling makes the writing task possible, albeit with some detriment to text quality.

One way in which processing resources can be conserved, therefore, is by adopting a simpler and qualitatively different writing strategy. Whether or not there are grounds for two distinct models, as Bereiter and Scardamalia argue, it is certainly the case that less experienced writers produce simpler texts. It seems probable that developmental differences in the complexity of texts produced map onto differences in the number of ideas that can be coordinated within the limits of the writer's short-term storage capacity (McCutchen and Perfetti, 1982).

A second way in which writing processes might be adapted to work within the limits of cognitive capacity is for writers to deliberately adopt strategies that reduce the number of processes that are active at any one time. Outlining in advance of producing full text, for example, has some benefits for text quality (Kellogg, 1988,

1990). This may be because it reduces the possibility of overload during drafting, although this effect does not appear to be present in more direct measures of cognitive load (Kellogg, 1988). Both Fayol, and Ransdell and Levy in their contributions to this book discuss strategies that writers might deliberately adopt to manage cognitive load. Fayol presents evidence that writers under increased cognitive load may simply slow down their rate of production. Specifically, adult writers are more successful at moderating the speed at which they transcribe so as to accommodate higher level, conceptual processes that are running simultaneously. Ransdell and Levy argue that resource flexibility - the ability to shift resource use between processes, and between processing and storage - is an important determinant of writing success.

Thirdly, the way in which writers' knowledge is structured will affect its use of short-term storage capacity. Miller (1956) argued that the number of items of information that are available to immediate processing is around seven but, crucially, that what constitutes an item will depend on how information is represented: sets of related concepts can be grouped together as a chunk and then represented in short term memory by a single label. The ability to chunk domain-specific information is an important feature of expertise (e.g., Chase and Simon, 1973; Patel and Groen, 1991). Assuming high level representations of the text, in the form of goals and plans, do play an important role in text production, then some mechanism like chunking will be necessary so that these can have meaning within short term memory. The item *writing strategies*, which is a feature of the mental plan that has guided the writing of this chapter, is only of use because it acts as a label for a much larger set of concepts. As we mentioned above, Ericsson and Kintsch (1995) go further in arguing that very well-learned information within long term memory can be directly accessible without making demands on short term storage capacity. Kellogg in his contribution to this volume presents some evidence for this being an important mechanism in writing.

How writers' knowledge is structured will, therefore, affect the extent to which the writing process loads cognitive resources. Defining a rhetorical problem, for example, for one task and then storing the solution in an easily accessible form will obviate the need to expend processing resources on repeating the process the next time a similar task is encountered. It may be that when discourse and content knowledge are well learned then the writing processes will be more similar to the knowledge telling than to knowledge transforming models, even for experienced, adult writers.

5   SUMMARY AND OVERVIEW

Text production has, therefore, the potential for being a very complex and resource demanding process. This means that in practice how writers process information to produce text is mediated by the limitations of cognitive resources. It is necessary, therefore, in developing models of the writing process to consider the cognitive costs both as a factor that directly affects the mapping between the writer's knowledge and the finished text and as setting limits on what processes might sensibly be hypothesised. The chapters that follow provide convincing evidence that the nature of the text that a writer produces is, in part, mediated by factors to do with resource use and limitations. Developmental and individual differences in text quality, for example, may be attributed in part to variation in cognitive capacity (e.g., Ransdell and Levy, 1996 and this volume; Swanson and Berninger, 1994). The implications of limited resources go beyond differences among writers, however, and may account directly for the way in which writers structure their text or construct their arguments (see, for example, Dansac and Alamargot, 1998). Because it is possible to identify a sequence of ideas in the text that a writer produces, there is a tendency to assume (a) that she had this particular sequence of ideas in mind when she wrote it, (b) that it was her intention that these particular ideas be communicated, and (c) that her cognitive processes must, therefore, be modelled in terms of her attempts to achieve this end. As we understand more of the processes by which text is produced we may well find that, regardless of the writer's communicative intention or of the meaning that the finished text conveys, its structure and content are at least partly mediated simply by the constraints imposed by the writer's limited cognitive capacity.

The chapters that follow present a detailed and well supported picture of the ways in which the writing process loads working memory. Taken together, they set an agenda for future debate and investigation that should keep psychologists with an interest in writing busy for a good long time. Each chapter describes a wealth of theory and research, much of which is lost in attempts to summarise them. However, since chapter overviews are a prototypical feature of the introductory chapter genre, we reluctantly outline the content of the book thus:

In *Chapter 2*, Fayol describes a large body of research exploring the processing demands of various sub-components of the writing process. He demonstrates that processes that are typically seen as being highly automatised in adult writers - lexical access, spelling, and handwriting - in fact have some cognitive costs that need to be managed by the writer. This suggests, therefore, that along side higher level processes - content generation, macrostructural planning and so forth - lower level processes also contribute to overall demand on cognitive resources. Fayol concludes by discussing how experienced writers manage cognitive demands through moment-by-moment variation of the pace of their writing.

In *Chapter 3* Levy and Marek set themselves the task of finding empirical evidence for claims made by Kellogg (1996) about the role of the phonological loop in the writing process. In a series of experiments that looked at writers listening to irrelevant speech while performing various tasks focusing on different components of the writing process, they found, consistent with Kellogg's claims, that translation of ideas into text appeared to be affected by irrelevant speech but that other components of the writing process were not. Interestingly, they also found evidence that, despite being placed under additional cognitive load, writers were able to modify their writing strategies so as to complete the writing tasks with a fair degree of success.

Kellogg, in *Chapter 4*, argues for the appropriateness of Baddeley's model of working memory to the understanding of processing demands in writing. In support of this he shows that on the basis of this theory it is possible to generate strong and testable hypotheses about the processing demands of different components of the writing process and how these will interact. In Kellogg's account, the central executive plays a vital role in most of the writing process, planning places particular demands on spatial component of working memory, and translating and reading place particular demands on the verbal component. He presents evidence suggesting that verbal and spatial processing resources are to some extent independent, and concludes that an account of working memory in writing needs at least to include these components. Finally, he also presents evidence that long-term working memory effects occur during text production, with writers with higher domain knowledge making less demand on cognitive resources.

Alongside the depth of the research evidence that Kellogg presents it is interesting that his chapter nurtures a mutually beneficial relationship between theories of writing and theories about working memory. This trend is continued in *Chapter 5* by Lea and Levy. After a useful and thorough overview of different accounts of working memory (in the more general sense of the term), they suggest a modified version of Baddeley's model as an account of working memory in writing. Specifically they argue, like Kellogg, that it is necessary to differentiate spatial and verbal processing resources in order to account for processing demand effects in writing. However, they suggest that these resources should be seen as flexible resource pools rather than the fixed structures hypothesised by Baddeley. They report three experiments which support these claims.

In *Chapter 6*, Negro and Chanquoy adopt a different approach to exploring the relationship between writing performance and processing capacity. They focus on a particular feature of writing performance, the fact that errors of agreement between noun and verb regularly occur in written French, and suggest a subtle and convincing explanation for their findings in terms of resource demands. This detailed exploration of a single psycholinguistic phenomenon is relatively common in research on oral production but rare in research on text production. This chapter illustrates the potential productivity of such an approach and, perhaps, points the way for more detailed testing of process models of writing.

Finally in *Chapter 7*, Ransdell and Levy present the findings of a series of studies exploring the relationship between various complex memory span measures and writing performance. As we discussed above, complex span measures provide a measure of the load placed by both storage and processing on working memory for a particular individual performing a specific task. Complex span thus provides a task-specific measure of overall cognitive load. They found that both writing span and reading span predict both reading ability and writing ability. This suggests that there are underlying, language-task specific differences in memory skill. Ransdell and Levy argue that these may be associated with the ability to flexibly allocate cognitive resources to the sub-processes where they are most needed.

> Just and Carpenter

AUTHOR NOTE

Correspondence concerning this chapter may be directed to Mark Torrance, Institute of Behavioural Sciences, University of Derby, Mickleover, Derby, DE3 5GX, UK (m.torrance@derby.ac.uk).

REFERENCES

Baddeley, A. (1990). *Human memory: theory and practice.* Hove, UK: Erlbaum.
Baddeley, A. (1993). Working memory or working attention? In A. Baddeley, & L. Weiskrantz (Ed.), *Attention: Selection, awareness and control. A tribute to Donald Broadbent* (pp. 152-170). Oxford: Oxford University Press.
Baddeley, A. D., & Hitch, G. (1974). Working memory. In G. H. Bower (Ed.), *The psychology of learning and motivation: Advances in research and theory* (vol. 8, pp. 281-301). London: Academic Press.

Bereiter, C., & Scardamalia, M. (1987). *The psychology of written composition*. Hillsdale, N.J.: Erlbaum.

Bereiter, C., Burtis, P. J., & Scardamalia, M. (1988). Cognitive operations in constructing main point in written composition. *Journal of memory and language, 27*, 261-278.

Bourdin, B. & Fayol, M. (1994). Is written production more difficult than oral production: A working memory approach. *International Journal of Psychology, 29*, 591-620.

Chase, W. G., & Simon, H. A. (1973). Perception in chess. *Cognitive psychology, 4*, 55-81.

Cohen, D. (1977). *Psychologists on psychology*. London: Routledge and Kegan Paul.

Daneman, M., & Carpenter, P. A. (1980). Individual differences in working memory and reading. *Journal of verbal learning and verbal behavior, 19*, 450-466.

Dansac, C., & Alamargot, D. (1998). Accessing referential information during text production: When and why. In M. Torrance, & D. Galbraith (Ed.), *Knowing what to write: Conceptual processes in text production*. Amsterdam: Amsterdam University Press.

Ericsson, K. A., & Kintsch, W. (1995). Long-term working memory. *Psychological Review, 102*, 211-245.

Flower, L. S., & Hayes, J. R. (1980a). The dynamics of composing: Making plans and juggling constraints. In L. W. Gregg, & E. R. Steinberg (Ed.), *Cognitive processes in writing* (pp. 31-50). Hillsdale, N.J.: Erlbaum.

Flower, L., & Hayes, J. (1980b). The cognition of discovery: Defining the rhetorical problem. *College Composition and Communication, 31*(2), 21-32.

Fodor, J. A. (1983). *The modularity of mind: An essay on faculty psychology*. Cambridge, Mass: MIT Press.

Galbraith, D. (1998). Writing as a knowledge constituting process. In M. Torrance, & D. Galbraith (Ed.), *Knowing what to write: Conceptual processes in text production*. Amsterdam: Amsterdam University Press.

Hartley, J., & Knapper, C. K. (1984). Academics and their writing. *Studies in Higher Education, 9*, 151-167.

Hayes, J. R. (1996). A new framework for understanding cognition and affect in writing. In C. M. Levy, & S. Ransdell (Ed.), *The science of writing: Theories, methods, individual differences, and applications* (pp. 1-26). Mahwah, N.J.: Erlbaum.

Hayes, J. R., & Flower, L. S. (1980). Identifying the organisation of writing processes. In L. Gregg, & E. R. Steinberg (Ed.), *Cognitive processes in writing* (pp.3-30). Hillsdale, N.J.: Erlbaum.

Jeffery, G. C., & Underwood, G. (1995, January). *The role of working memory in sentence production*. Paper presented at the annual meeting of the British Experimental Psychology Society, London.

Kellogg, R. T (1988). Attentional overload and writing performance: effects of rough draft and outline strategies. *Journal of experimental psychology: Learning, memory and cognition, 14*(2), 355-365.

Kellogg, R. T. (1987). Effects of topic knowledge on the allocation of processing time and cognitive effort to writing processes. *Memory and Cognition, 15*(3), 256-266.

Kellogg, R. T. (1990). Effectiveness of prewriting strategies as a function of task demands. *American journal of psychology, 103*(3), 327-342.

Kellogg, R. T. (1996). A model of working memory in writing. In C. M. Levy, & S. Ransdell (Ed.), *The Science of Writing: Theories, methods, individual differences and applications* (pp. 57-71). Mahwah, N.J.: Erlbaum.

Levy, R., & Ransdell, S. (1995). Is writing as difficult as it seems? *Memory and Cognition, 23*, 767-779.

Logie, R. H. (1996). The seven ages of working memory. In J. T. E. Richardson (Ed.), *Working memory and human cognition* (pp. 31-65). Oxford: Oxford University Press.

Lowenthal, D., & Wason, P. C. (1977,). Academics and their writing. *Times Literary Supplement*, pp. 781.

McCutchen, D. (1996). A capacity theory of writing: Working memory in composition. *Educational psychology review, 8*, 299-325.

McCutchen, D., & Perfetti, C. (1982). Coherence and connectedness in the development of discourse production. *Text, 2*, 113-139.

Miller, G. A. (1956). The magical number seven, plus or minus two: Some limits on our capacity for processing information. *Psychological review, 93*, 81-97.

Newell, A., & Simon, H. A. (1972). *Human problem solving*. London: Prentice Hall.

Patel, V. L., & Groen, G. J. (1991). The general and specific nature of medical expertise: a critical look. In K. A. Ericsson, & J. Smith (Ed.), *Toward a general theory of expertise* (pp. 93-125). Cambridge: Cambridge University Press.

Plimpton, G. (1965). *Writers at work: The Paris Review interviews.* New York: Viking.

Ransdell, S., & Levy, C. M. (1996). Working memory constraints on writing quality and fluency. In C. M. Levy, & S. Ransdell (Ed.), *The science of writing: theories, methods, individual differences, and applications* (pp. 93-107). Mahwah, N.J.: Erlbaum.

Richardson, J. T. E. (1996). Evolving concepts of working memory. In J. T. E. Richardson (Ed.), *Working memory and human cognition* (pp. 3-30). Oxford: Oxford University Press.

Scardamalia, M., & Bereiter, C. (1991). Literate expertise. In K. A. Ericsson, & J. Smith (Ed.), *Toward a general theory of expertise: Prospects and limits* (pp. 172-194). Cambridge: Cambridge University Press.

Schilperoord, J. (1996). *It's about time: Temporal aspects of cognitive processes in text production.* Amsterdam: Rodopi.

Schilperoord, J., & Sanders, T. (1998). How hierarchical text structure affects retrieval processes: Implications of pause and text analysis. In M. Torrance, & D. Galbraith (Ed.), *Knowing what to write: Conceptual processes in text production.* Amsterdam: Amsterdam University Press.

Schumacher, G. M., Scott, B. T., Klare, G. R., Cronin, F. C., & Lambert, D. A. (1989). Cognitive processes in journalistic genres. *Written communication, 6,* 390-407.

Stanovich, K. E. (1990). Concepts in developmental theories of reading. *Developmental Review, 10,* 72-100.

Swanson, H. L., & Beringer, V. W. (1994). Working memory as a source of individual differences in children's writing. In J. S. Carlson, & E. C. Butterfield (Ed.), *Advances in cognition and educational practice* (vol. 2: Children's writing: Toward a process theory of the development of skilled writing, pp. 31-56). Greenwich, C.T.: JAI Press.

Torrance, M. (1996a). Is writing expertise like other kinds of expertise. In G. Rijlaarsdam, H. van den Bergh, & M. Couzijn (Ed.), *Theories, models and methodology in writing research* (pp. 3-9). Amsterdam: Amsterdam University Press.

Torrance, M. (1996b). Strategies for familiar writing tasks: Case studies of undergraduates writing essays. In G. Rijlaarsdam, H. van den Bergh, & M. Couzijn (Ed.), *Theories, models and methodology in writing research* (pp. 283-298). Amsterdam: Amsterdam University Press.

Torrance, M., Thomas, G. V., & Robinson, E. J. (1996). Finding something to write about: Strategic and automatic processes in idea generation. In M. Levy, & S. Ransdell (Ed.), *The Science of Writing.* Mahwah, N.J.: Erlbaum.

Torrance, M., Thomas, G. V., & Robinson, E. J. (in press). Individual differences in the writing behaviour of undergraduate students. British Journal of Educational Psychology.

van Waes, L. (1992). The influence of the computer on writing profiles. In P. Maat, & M. Steehouder (Ed.), *Studies of functional text quality* (pp. 173-186). Amsterdam: Rodopi.

van Wijk, C. (1998). Conceptual process in argumentation: A developmental perspective. In M. Torrance, & D. Galbraith (Ed.), *Knowing what to write: Conceptual processes in text production.* Amsterdam: Amsterdam University Press.

From on-line management problems to strategies in written composition

Michel Fayol

L.E.A.D. / C.N.R.S., University of Bourgogne, France

ABSTRACT

When composing texts, people have to deal with the management of several component skills which have to be coordinated to produce a coherent and cohesive text adapted to an audience. As most of the subcomponents make some demands on cognitive resources, increasing the cost of lower-level processes may decrease the performance of higher-level processes, and vice versa. As a consequence, to reach the goal of composing good texts, people have to find some ways of managing such situations: automating some skills; combining strategies; allocating more or less time and effort to deal with a particular subcomponent. Several examples are provided and the results are discussed in the framework of an adaptive strategy choice conception of composing.

1   INTRODUCTION

Probably, the main problem children and adults are faced with in written composition concerns the on-line management of several subcomponent skills which have to be coordinated in order to reach the goal: namely, to produce a coherent and cohesive text adapted to an audience. Regarding this problem, two points are worth noting. First, composing is a complex task which needs to be decomposed into subcomponents to be studied. Most, if not all, of these subcomponents make some cognitive demands and have access to a general limited pool of cognitive resources. Second, writers adapt to manage the competing demands of different subcomponents. In the following paper, this conception will be discussed and some empirical evidence will be provided in its support.

2   COMPOSING AS A COMPLEX TASK INVOLVING COSTLY COMPONENTS

Human beings have a limited pool of general cognitive resources (including attention and working memory) that can be flexibly allocated to accommodate the real-time needs of the processing system. In general, the allocation of resources is focused; that is, it is centred upon a topic and upon processes especially relevant for the task at hand. As composing is a goal-directed activity, most resources are devoted to the global control of the production processes (Herrmann & Grabowski, 1995). This controlled processing demands focused attention and conscious mental effort. It is slow, and deals with serially organized information because it is either impossible or very difficult to execute different operations simultaneously (Brown & Carr, 1989; Jensen & Whang, 1994). However, in order to achieve the goal, the writer has to exert different component subskills such as transcribing or grammatical encoding (Bock & Levelt, 1994). Under certain task conditions, an inefficient subcomponent can disrupt performance because it draws resources away from focused activities. Such disruptions can affect either higher-order components or lower-level processes.

Composing is a complex task which requires the efficient on-line coordination of both lower-level processes such as graphic transcription, lexical access, syntactic frame construction (Bock & Levelt, 1994; Levelt, 1989) and higher-level processes such as elaborating ideas and conceptual relations, thematic processing, maintaining coherence and cohesion and respecting text-type constraint processes (Berninger & Swanson, 1994; Fayol, 1991 a, 1991 b, 1997). We assume that all these processes have a cognitive cost, although in some cases this might be very low, as discussed later. However, some processes can become easier to manage because they can be automated.

2.1 How the cost of lower-level processes impairs the performance of higher-level components

The cost of the graphic transcription processes
Zesiger (1995) has shown that the graphic transcription of letters and words moves from a slow, irregular and highly controlled process in young children to a fast, regular and mainly automatic process in adults. As a consequence, its cost is reduced and adults are generally not impaired in the management of higher-order activities when they have to deal with them in the written rather than in the oral modality. This is not the case for young children who have automated the production of oral language, but not written language. Bourdin and Fayol (1993, 1994, 1996) have shown that, in both a serial recall task of unrelated words and in a sentence production task, the performance of 7-8 year-old children, but not that of adults, was impaired in the written modality compared with the oral modality. This result suggested that the cognitive cost of writing hampered the maintenance of information in working memory in children. In contrast, the same phenomenon did not occur in the oral modality due to the high automaticity of the production processes. To support this hypothesis, Bourdin and Fayol were able to show that adults' performance decreased dramatically when they had to write using capital letters. Using a rarely practised graphic subsystem increased the load of the transcription process and led to a decrease in memory performance. Overloading a lower-level component through increasing the difficulty of managing the output modality was thus shown to affect a higher-level component, the maintaining and recalling of a series of items (Figure 1).

The cost of lexical access
Another example comes from the study of the production of words in the oral as well as in the written modality. The frequency effect in word naming is well known: naming objects takes more time when the lexical labels are rare than when these labels are frequent (Levelt, 1989). This explains at least partially the variations of between-word pauses and hesitations in oral production (Holmes, 1995; Goldman-Eisler, 1972). However, until recently, very few data were available concerning the writing of isolated words. Writing words raises two problems. First, people have to access a mental lexicon, and we do not know whether or not this lexicon is the same as the one which is involved in oral production (see neuropsychological evidence in

Figure 1   *Proportions of words recalled by adults as a function of output modality (oral vs. lower-case letters vs. capital letters). (from Bourdin & Fayol, 1994, Experiment 3b).*

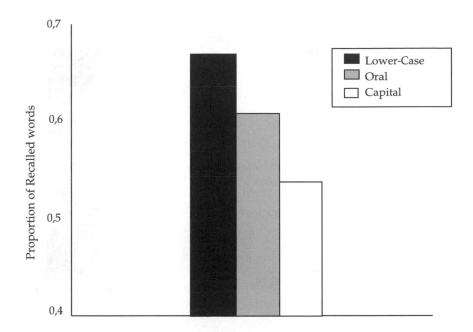

Caramazza, 1997). Second, writing words necessitates lexical spelling, the difficulty of which varies from one language to another depending on the familiarity and regularity of phoneme-grapheme correspondences (Kreiner, 1996).

Regarding these two problems, Bonin et al. (Bonin, 1997; Bonin, Fayol & Gombert, 1997) studied the naming and writing of the same nouns on the basis of pictures depicting well-known objects. The nouns were either frequent or rare (according to Content, Mousty & Radeau, 1990), and the dependent variable was the time needed by the participants to produce the words. The results showed (1) that as usual, latencies were longer in writing than in naming; an effect that was probably due to the planning and execution of the graphemic dimensions and (2) that word frequency affected writing as well as naming from pictures (Figure 2). Several control experiments ruled out the possibility that this effect could be due to identification of pictures or to post-lexical processes. Lexical production is thus a costly process in the written as well as in the oral modality. Its cost depends on the difficulty of retrieving more or less frequent or familiar words from memory but not on the output modality, oral or written.

The cost of spelling irregularities
Spelling difficulties also have an impact on the cost of writing. Bourdin and Fayol (1994) studied the effect of lexical spelling difficulties, indexed through familiarity and regularity of phoneme-grapheme correspondence, on the serial recall of word series in third grade children and adults. Children and adults were presented with series of words (of five letters and one or two syllables), familiar or not, regularly

Figure 2   *Mean median latencies (in ms) as a function of output modality (oral production vs. writing) and frequency (high frequency [HF] vs. low frequency [LF]) in noun production from pictures (From Bonin, 1995).*

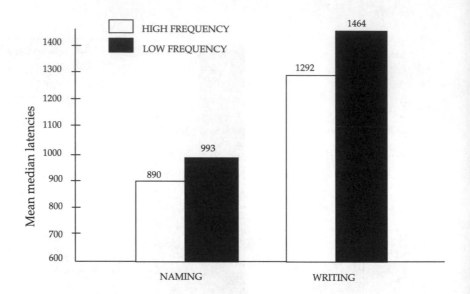

Figure 3   *Proportions of recalled words as a function of recall mode (oral vs. written) and of word characteristics (Regular and Familiar [RF]; Regular and Unfamiliar [RU]; Irregular and Familiar [IF]; Irregular and Unfamiliar [IU]) in adults (From Bourdin & Fayol, 1994, Experiment 4).*

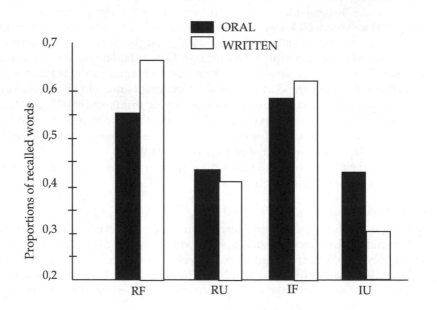

spelled or not. There were thus four categories of words: Familiar and Regular; Familiar and Irregular; Unfamiliar and Regular; Unfamiliar and Irregular. Participants were asked to recall these words either in the oral or in the written modality. As expected (1) the more familiar the words, the better the recall, in adults and children alike and (2) a regularity effect showed up with children as well as with adults (see Figure 3). Irregular words were significantly less well recalled than familiar and/or regular words but only under the written modality, as expected. While word familiarity influenced recall performance in the oral as well as in the written modality, word regularity had an impact in the written output only (Kreiner, 1996). Spelling difficulties thus increase the cost of writing.

In the previous examples, increasing the cost of lower-level processes decreased the performance of higher-level processes. However, the reverse could be true. When more resources have to be devoted to higher-level processes, the functioning of lower-level processes can also be impaired or disrupted.

2.2 How the cost of higher-level processes can impair the performance on lower-level processes.

Disrupting graphic transcription.
Rather surprisingly, in a pilot study Kalsbeek (1965) found that severely increasing the difficulties in the management of higher-order processes could impair even the quality of graphic transcriptions in adults. When participants were asked to man-

Figure 4   Proportion of agreement errors as a function of load (sentences vs. sentences + memory load) and first and second position noun number (from Fayol et al., 1994).

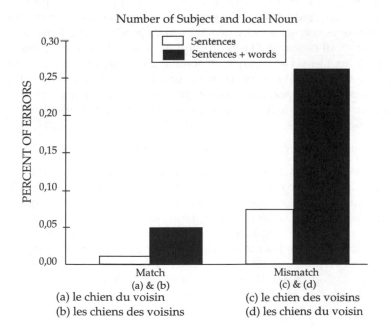

age both an auditory comprehension task and a written production task, their graphic transcription became more and more impaired when the difficulty of processing was increased by the experimenter. This is a very interesting result concerning the fragility of what is generally considered as a highly automated skill: even the written transcription process can be severely impaired when the cost of the activities to coordinate become impossible to manage.

Inducing spelling errors.
Fayol, Largy and Lemaire (1994) and Largy, Fayol and Lemaire (1996) have induced agreement errors on verbs in highly educated adults writing down orally presented sentences. Probably due to the silent characteristics of written French morphology, adults were led to inflect erroneously verbs such as *arrive* when they had to both write a sentence like *Le chien des voisins arrive* (literally "The dog of the neighbours arrives") and temporarily store a series of five words in Working Memory. They wrote *arrivent* instead of *arrive*, making the verb agree with the closest (local) noun instead of making the correct subject-verb agreement (Figure 4).

The same phenomenon occurred in children's production. Totereau, Thévenin and Fayol (1997) have shown that French children were able to use the relevant noun and verb inflections when explicitly asked to do so. However, they "forgot" to add these inflections when they had to recall (by writing down) the same linguistic patterns or to produce them when they composed a text.

2.3 Summary

Disruptions can thus occur both in a bottom-up and in a top-down way. In the first case the cost of lower-level processes hampers the management of higher-level processes. In the second case, the resources devoted to higher-level processes prevent the correct realization of lower-level processes.

All the above-mentioned dimensions of written composition, graphic transcription, lexical access, and spelling, can be more or less automatic. Such automation leads to the reduction of capacity demands with practice, and thus increases the ability to carry out concurrent tasks. In contrast, some other dimensions persist as problem-solving tasks. For example, in accessing and organising ideas, the writer must exert conscious and careful control over what she or he is doing. The cost of such higher-order activities can be only slightly reduced through practice. As a consequence, the writer has to find some ways of managing such situations.

3   ON THE COORDINATION OF COMPONENT SKILLS IN COMPOSING

The coordination of the different subcomponents can proceed in a number of different ways. At least two different mechanisms can be involved in the reduction of costs necessary to make composition tasks manageable. The first mechanism is automaticity, which exploits the constancy of either task information or task operations, for example, by strengthening the internode associations between components of a skill such as producing sequences of graphemes or using particular syntactic frames (Anderson, 1983, 1995; Brown & Carr, 1989; Logan, 1988; Logan et Klapp, 1991; MacKay, 1982). The other mechanism has to do with task combination strategies (Brown & Carr, 1989). It involves changes over time in the relations between the task components that are combined. For example, attention switching exploits the possibilities of flexibly allocating cognitive resources as a function of the capacity demands of performance. Such a strategy enables finely adapted moves from parallel to serial organisation (Broadbent, 1982).

3.1 Automaticity and its limits

When a component skill is automated, it becomes faster, effortless and non-interfering. As a consequence, it can deal with relatively large amounts of information and it is possible to perform various operations simultaneously. When certain information and/or processing skills have become automated, they do not overload the limited capacity of the working memory system. However, this automaticity is not an all-or-nothing phenomenon (Logan & Klapp, 1991). Practice effects can be observed even after automaticity is achieved. Over training beyond automaticity leads to limited but significantly reliable gains in speed and, more importantly, to a dramatic reduction in interference from concurrent tasks (Klapp, Boches, Trabert & Logan, 1991). Consequently, the more it is over trained, the more an automatic skill can be conducted in parallel with another activity. For example, automatising writing enables writers to devote more and more resources to retrieving lexical items from memory. However, even when activities are (relatively) automated, people can simultaneously carry out only a limited number of them. When two activities can occur simultaneously within the "band-width" of the limited capacity, it is difficult to determine their respective and total cost. It is necessary to use secondary tasks (Kellogg, 1987a, 1987b, 1994; Power, 1985, 1986) and to measure reaction times (RT). In these experiments, it is assumed that the more resources are devoted to the main activities, the longer the RT to the secondary task is.

3.2 Adapting the production rhythm

When writers encounter limited difficulties in integrating subcomponent skills in real time, they adjust their writing speed by decreasing transcription rates and/or by increasing pause duration. They thus use task combination strategies. For example, Chanquoy, Foulin and Fayol (1990) have shown that adults, but not 8 year-olds, modified their between-clause pause durations and that adults varied their within-clause writing rate as a function of the predictability of the events they were reporting in a story (Table 1). These results suggest that adults are able to perform graphic

Table 1   Distribution of time parameters in third graders and adults in a text continuation task (adapted from Chanquoy, Foulin & Fayol, 1990).

	Pre-writing pauses (seconds)	Between clause pauses (seconds)	Within clause writing rate (characters per second)
Adults			
Expected endings	8.26	5.97	2.75
Unexpected endings	13.51	8.96	2.57
3rd *Graders*			
Expected endings	7.97	7.8	1.08
Unexpected endings	9.67	8.0	1.04

transcription concurrently with some other higher-level activities and, thus, to adjust the rhythms of the lower-level activities to the changing demands of conceptual and/or linguistic operations. In contrast, young children were not able to modify their writing speed flexibly, probably due to the fact that writing activities are still demanding at that age (see Bourdin & Fayol, 1994).

In order to better estimate the weight of the higher-level components in pause and rate variations, Fayol and Stephant (1991) compared the written composition speed with the written recall speed of the same two-clause story endings, as produced by 9-year-olds and by adults. By subtracting pause durations and transcription rates in recall from the same parameters in composition, it was possible to assess the distribution of the costs of conceptual and/or linguistic activities within and between clauses at every point in the text. The main result was that, when composing the last clause of a story, adults wrote as fast as when recalling this clause, which was not the case with the previous clauses. This result suggests that adults plan the to-be-transcribed clause (n) when they are writing down the previous one (n-1). Children's performance differed strikingly from this pattern: both between and within clause pauses were longer in composition than in recall, whatever their positions in the story endings. These data suggest that conceptual-linguistic and transcription operations are too costly to be conducted in parallel by 9 year-olds. Children would thus proceed by alternating activities, first planning then formulating then transcribing; the cost being so high that they could only produce texts following a step-by-step procedure (i.e., the knowledge telling strategy; Scardamalia & Bereiter, 1982).

3.3 The strategic allocation of resources

Sometimes it is impossible to conduct two (or more) activities in parallel. When the writer becomes aware of this difficulty, he can delay one of them and focus on the other(s), strategically allocating more or less time and effort to managing his own production (Levy & Ransdell, 1995; Scardamalia & Bereiter, 1991). The more efficient the time and effort sharing, the better the text quality (Levy & Ransdell, 1995). However, even if the distribution of the main writing components over time is (relatively) easy to organise, people, even experts, are sometimes unable to deal with specific problems, due to temporary overload.

Even though the language production process in adults is highly automated it may become disrupted when they have to deal with a secondary task. Comparing the performance of a recall task under normal vs. divided attention conditions, Jou & Harris (1992) reported that, under the divided attention condition, less information was recalled together with increased speech defects and pause durations (cf. also Fayol, Largy & Lemaire, 1994; Largy, Fayol & Lemaire, 1996).

4   CONCLUSION

At any single point in time during writing, people have to deal with the management of several subcomponent skills. Improvement of this management can be obtained by automating some skills (graphic transcription, spelling, agreement; e.g., McCutchen's automatic processes, 1988), by increasing the knowledge and processing of some highly stereotyped situations (story schemas, chains of anaphoric references; see, for example, McCutchen's fluent processes, Fayol, 1991 b; Fayol &

Lemaire, 1993) and, obviously, by having a well structured knowledge base about the topic dealt with in the text. However, due to the very nature of written composition, writers, even experts, are inescapably subjected to overload, because planning and revising are always cognitively costly. To cope with such a costly situation, they have to develop adaptive strategy choices (Siegler, 1986, Siegler & Shipley, 1995). That is, people vary their choice of procedure in response to problem difficulties (are they highly knowledgeable about the topic?), changes in their own competencies (how costly are transcription and spelling?), task instructions (is it important to focus on spelling?), and so on. In the future, we will have to examine whether and when children become efficient enough in transcribing to modulate their writing rate and to simultaneously write and plan ahead part of what they have to report. We will then have to study how children (and adults) modify their strategy choices (plan extensively before beginning to compose or immediately start composing and pause regularly and at length between successive sentences) as a function of their experience and of the constraints of the situation. This will enable us to draw conclusions that have implications for the way in which writing is taught.

AUTHOR NOTE

The author wishes to thank Lucile Chanquoy and Eric Esperet for their helpful comments on an earlier draft of this chapter. Correspondence regarding this chapter can be directed to the author at LAPSCO/CNRS, Université Blaise Pascal, 34 avenue Carnot, 63000 Clermont Ferrand, France.

REFERENCES

Anderson, J.R. (1983). *The architecture of cognition*. Cambridge, MA: Harvard University Press.
Anderson, J.R. (1995). *Learning and memory*. New-York: John Wiley & Sons, Inc.
Berninger, V.W. & Swanson, H.L. (1994). Modifying Hayes and Flower's model of skilled writing to explain beginning and developing writing . In E. Butterfield (Ed.), *Children's writing: Toward a process theory of skilled writing*. Greenwich, C.T.: J.A.I. Press.
Bock, J.K. & Levelt, W.J.M. (1994). Grammatical encoding. In M.A. Gernsbacher (Ed.), *Handbook of psycholinguistics*. New-York: Academic Press.
Bonin, P. (1995). *Accès lexical en production verbale: Essai de mise en évidence d'une spécificité de l'écrit*. Unpublished doctoral dissertation, Université of Bourgogne, France.
Bonin, P. (1997). Produire des mots isolés, oralement et par écrit. Etudes de Linguistique appliquée, 7, 29-70.
Bonin, P., Fayol, M. & Gombert, J.E. (1997). The role of phonological and orthographic codes in picture naming and writing. *Current Psychology of Cognition, 16*, 299-324.
Bourdin, B. & Fayol, M. (1994). Is written production more difficult than oral production: A working memory approach. *International Journal of Psychology, 29*, 591-620.
Bourdin, B. & Fayol, M. (1996). Mode effect in a sentence production task. *CPC/Current Psychology of Cognition, 15*, 245-264.
Bourdin, B., & Fayol, M. (1993). Comparing oral and written language production: A working memory approach. In G. Eigler & T. Jechle (Eds.), *Writing: Current trends in European research*. Hochschlul: Verlag.
Broadbent, D.E. (1982). Task combination and the selective intake of information. *Acta Psychologica, 50*, 253-290.

Brown, T.L. & Carr, T.H. (1989). Automaticity in skill acquisition: Mechanisms for reducing interference in concurrent performance. *Journal of Experimental Psychology: Human Perception and Performance, 15,* 686-700.

Caramazza, A. (1997). How many levels of processing are-there in lexical access? Cognitive Neu-
ropsychology, 14, 177-208.

Chanquoy, L., Foulin, J.N., & Fayol, M. (1990). The on-line management of short text written by
children and adults. *C.P.C/European Bulletin of Cognitive Psychology, 10,* 513-540.

Content, A., Mousty, P. & Radeau, M. (1990). Brulex: Une base de donnée lexicale informatisée pour
le français écrit et parlé. *L'Année Psychologique, 90,* 551-566.

Fayol, M. & Stephant, I. (1991). Assessing cognitive load in writing. Communication at the Fourth
conference of the European Association for Research on Learning and Instruction. Turku, Fin-
land. August, 24-28.

Fayol, M. (1991a). From sentence production to text production: Investigating fundamental processes. *European Journal of Psychology of Education, 6,* 101-119.

Fayol, M. (1991b). Text typologies: A cognitive approach. In G. Denhière & J.P. Rossi (Eds.), *Text and
text processing.* Amsterdam: North Holland.

Fayol, M. (1994). From declarative and procedural knowledge to the management of declarative
and procedural knowledge. *European Journal of Psychology of Education, 9,* 179-190.

Fayol, M. (1997). *Des idées du texte.* Paris: Presses Universitaires de France.

Fayol, M., & Lemaire, P. (1993). Levels of approach to discourse. In H.H. Brownell & Y. Joannette
(Eds.), *Alternative perspectives on the neuro-psychology of narrative discourse.* San Diego, CA: Singular Publishing Group.

Fayol, M., Largy, P., & Lemaire, P. (1994). When cognitive overload enhances subject-verb agreement errors. *The Quarterly Journal of Experimental Psychology, 47A,* 437-464.

Goldman-Eisler, F. (1972). Pauses, clauses and sentences. *Language and Speech, 15,* 103-113.

Herrmann, T. & Grabowski, J. (1995). Pre-terminal levels of process in oral and written language
production. In U.M. Quasthoff (Ed.), *Aspects of oral communication.* Berlin, G: Walter de Gruyter.

Holmes, V.M. (1995). A cross-linguistic comparison of the production of utterances in discourse.
Cognition, 54, 169-207.

Jensen, A.R. & Whang, P. A. (1994). Speed of accessing arithmetic facts in long-term memory: A
comparison of chinese-american and anglo-american children. *Contemporary Educational Psychology, 19,* 1-12.

Jou, J. & Harris, R.J. (1992). The effect of divided attention on speech production. *Bulletin of the
Psychonomic Society, 30,* 301-304.

Just, M. A. & Carpenter, P.A. (1992). A capacity theory of comprehension: Individual differences in
working memory. *Psychological Review, 99,* 122-149.

Kalsbeek, J.W.H. (1965). Mesure objective de la surcharge mentale. *Le Travail Humain, 28,* 121-132.

Kellogg, R.T. (1987a). Effects of topic knowledge on the allocation of processing time and cognitive
effort to writing processes. *Memory & Cognition, 15,* 256-266.

Kellogg, R.T. (1987b). Writing performance: Effects of cognitive strategies. *Written Communication,*
4, 269-298.

Kellogg, R.T. (1994). *The psychology of writing.* Oxford, UK: Oxford University Press.

Klapp, S.T. Boches, C.A. Trabert, M.L. & Logan G.D. (1991). Automatizing alphabet arithmetic. Are
there practice effects after automaticity is achieved? *Journal of Experimental Psychology: Learning,
Memory and Cognition, 17,* 196-209.

Kreiner, D.S. (1996). Effects of word familiarity and phoneme-grapheme polygraphy on oral spelling time and accuracy. *The Psychological Record, 46,* 49-70.

Largy, P., Fayol, M. & Lemaire, P. (1996). The homophone effect in written French: The case of
noun-verb inflection errors. *Language and Cognitive Processes, 10,* 217-255.

Levy, C.M. & Ransdell, S; (1995) Is writing as difficult as it seems? *Memory and Cognition, 23,* 767-
779.

Logan G.D. & Klapp, ST (1991) Automatizing alphabet arithmetic: I. Is extended practice necessary
to produce automaticity? *Journal of Experimental Psychology: Learning Memory and Cognition, 17,*
179-195.

Logan, G.D. (1988). Automaticity, resources and memory. *Human Factors, 30,* 883-914.

MacKay, D.G. (1982). The problem of flexibility, fluency, and speed-accuracy trade-off in killed behavior. *Psychological Review, 89*, 483-506.

McCutchen, D. (1988). Functional automaticity in children's writing. *Written Communication, 5*, 306-324.

McCutchen, D. (1995). Cognitive processes in children's writing: Developmental and individual differences. *Issues in Education, 1*, 123-160.

Penningroth, S.L. & Rosenfeld, S. (1995). Effects of high information processing load on the writing process and the story written. *Applied Psycholinguistics, 16*, 189-210.

Power, M.J. (1985). Sentence production and working memory. *The Quarterly Journal of Experimental Psychology, 37A*, 367-385.

Power, M.J. (1986). A technique for measuring processing load during speech production. *Journal of Psycholinguistic Research, 15*, 371-382.

Scardamalia , M. & Bereiter, C. (1982). Assimilative processes in composition planning. *Educational Psychologist, 17*, 165-171.

Scardamalia , M. & Bereiter, C. (1991). Literate expertise. In K.A. Ericsson and J. Smith (Eds.), *Towards a general theory of expertise*. Cambridge, MA: Cambridge University Press.

Siegler, R.S. & Shipley, C. (1995). Variation, selection, and cognitive change. In G. Halford and T. Simon (Eds.), *Developing cognitive competence: New approaches to process modelling*. Hillsdale, NJ: Erlbaum.

Siegler, R.S. (1986). Unities in thinking across domains in children's strategy choices. M. Perlmutter (Ed.), *Perspective for intellectual development: Minnesota symposium on child development*. Hillsdale, NJ: Erlbaum.

Totereau, C., Thevenin, M.G., & Fayol, M. (1997). The development of the understanding of number morphology in written French. In C. Perfetti, L. Rieben, and M. Fayol (Eds.), *Learning to spell*. Hillsdale, NJ: Erlbaum.

Zesiger, P. (1995). *Ecrire*. Paris: Presses Universitaires de France.

Testing Components of Kellogg's Multicomponent Model of Working Memory in Writing: The Role of the Phonological Loop

C. Michael Levy & **Pamela Marek**
University of Florida, USA

ABSTRACT

Kellogg's (1996) multicomponent theory of writing links text production processes to the working memory constructs (central executive aided by a visuospatial sketchpad and a phonological loop) proposed by Baddeley and his associates. This chapter describes five experiments designed to empirically assess some of the claims made by this theory regarding the role of the phonological loop or, more generally, a verbal subsystem of working memory in the production of text. That system is postulated to influence translating and reading processes during writing, but not planning, motor programming, response execution, or editing. The results obtained in the present experiment are largely supportive of Kellogg's claims regarding the involvement of a phonological loop construct in the production of text.

1 INTRODUCTION

During the last few years we have seen a flurry of research activity (for example, Johnson, Linton, & Madigan, 1994; Madigan, Johnson, & Linton, 1994; Ransdell & Levy, 1996a, b) and theoretical statements about the role of working memory in writing. On the theoretical side, Hayes (1996), Grabowski (1996), and Kellogg (1996; this volume) have each laid out new models of writing that rely heavily on the contributions of working memory. Each of these models derives in part from Baddeley's influential ideas about working memory processing.

Baddeley's model evolved from evidence suggesting that the unitary short-term store in the modal model (for example, Atkinson & Shriffrin, 1968) did not fit adequately with neurological data indicating that impairments in short-term store did not necessarily imply deficits in long-term learning. About 25 years ago, Baddeley and Hitch reported a series of studies aimed at determining the configuration of the short-term store thought to underlie performance in a range of cognitive tasks. In their now classic dual-task paradigm, which required a subject to perform a secondary task such as concurrently processing digits while doing some other, primary task, they demonstrated the involvement of working memory in reasoning and prose comprehension. Interestingly, while performance in the reasoning and comprehension tasks declined compared with control conditions, the decrement was not catastrophic. This suggested that the digits may have been held in a sub-system that was linked to a central processor which enabled the individual to experience only a little drain on central resources. These findings led to the development of a tripartite model of working memory, including a central executive and two slave subsystems, that is illustrated in Figure 1.

Figure 1   *A representation of a portion of Baddeley's model of working memory, adapted*
         from Gathercole and Baddeley (1993).

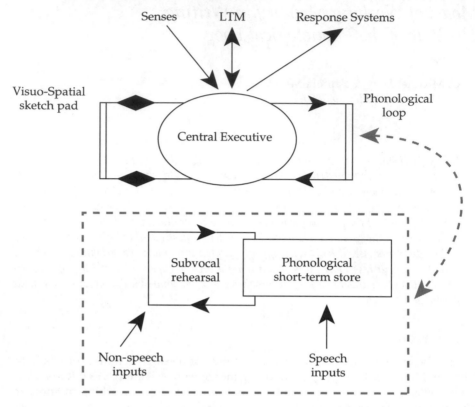

The basic ideas are straightforward and intuitively appealing. First, there is a central executive, which Baddeley and his associates claimed was responsible for regulating and coordinating the operations of a limited capacity working memory, directing input to the two slave systems, and retrieving information from long-term memory. They suggested that the central executive is an attentional controller and offered it as a link to conscious awareness. The central executive is served by two slave subsystems. One of these, the phonological loop, is designed for both storage and processing. The storage component holds a rapidly decaying memory trace in phonological code. An articulatory loop recycles and rehearses information to maintain it in the store, and also recodes visual information to enable it access to the store. The second slave system, the visuo-spatial sketchpad, is specialized for maintaining and processing visual or spatial information. Over the years, Baddeley and his associates have had a great deal to say about these systems, and these ideas are central to Kellogg's (1966) model of writing processes that is represented in Figure 2. Although Kellogg has elaborated and modified this model in the present volume, the research presented in this chapter applies to both the earlier and the current versions.

*Figure 2   A representation of Kellogg's extension of Baddeley's model of working memory
to writing. Adapted from Kellogg (1996).*

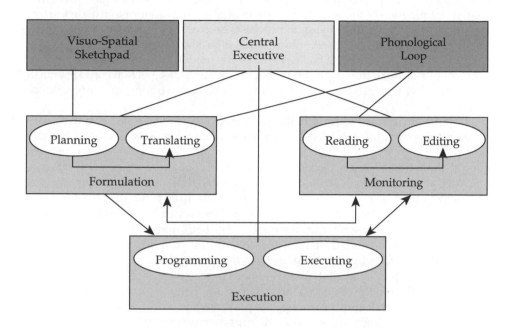

Kellogg maintained that three primary writing processes – formulation, execution
and monitoring – demand access to working memory. These processes, however,
place differential demands on working memory and involve different components
of memory. *Formulation* includes both goal-directed planning and organizational
activities. It also includes translating, which involves the transformation of these
plans into actual sentences. The planning subprocess draws on the visuo-spatial
sketchpad, while translating involves the phonological loop. Both formulation
subprocesses require the services of the central executive.

   Execution includes programming of motor movements as well as their overt execution. The programming subcomponent uses central executive resources, but executing, in adult writers, is considered automatic.

   The third subprocess, *Monitoring*, spans reading, which draws upon word recognition and comprehension skills. It also draws upon editing when writers compare what they wrote with what they intended to say. Reading calls upon both the
central executive and phonological loop, but Kellogg claims that editing involves
only resources in the central executive. This chapter describes five experiments that
attempt to find support for Kellogg's claims about the role of the phonological loop
in text production.

   How can the basic premises of this model be tested? Although there are many
ways to begin, our efforts have been directed towards two fundamentally distinct
approaches. In one of them, we follow in the tradition of the supporters and critics
(for example, Jones, 1995, LeCompte, 1996; Ransdell & Levy, 1996a) of the Baddeley

model of working memory by delivering tasks to participants that are designed to selectively and differentially load separate components of the central executive and its slave subsystems. In the second approach, our focus shifts to a much more molecular examination of the writing process in studies that attempt to isolate the formulation, monitoring and execution processes so that they can be examined independently. In both cases, however, our initial efforts were focused on designs that might permit support for the basic claims of the model. A more complete evaluation, which is beyond the scope of this chapter, requires designs that could establish that certain writing processes do not draw on certain working memory components.

To illustrate our first approach, Ransdell and Levy (1996a) noted that irrelevant unattended speech impairs memory performance and also slows writing production (Baddeley, 1986; Madigan, Johnson, & Linton, 1994). Unattended irrelevant speech slows and disrupts reasoning, comprehension, and memory performance and such effects have been attributed to the phonological loop component of working memory (Baddeley & Hitch, 1974; Baddeley, Thomson, & Buchanan, 1975; Colle & Welsh, 1976; Gathercole & Baddeley, 1993; Salame & Baddeley, 1982) and to temporal distinctiveness (Glenberg & Swanson, 1986; LeCompte, 1996).

In Baddeley's account, irrelevant speech prevents or limits access to rehearsal through the phonological or articulatory loop, which causes less overall working memory capacity to be available for the main processing task. In this view, these constraints will limit the amount of articulatory and phonological processing possible when a concurrent auditory message is played while writing. Limiting the availability of the phonological loop should disrupt mainly translating and reading, and thus influence writers' fluency. Accordingly, to manipulate the demands on the phonological loop, Ransdell and Levy (1996a) presented or withheld irrelevant speech while writers composed. They also altered the load on the central executive by interrupting writers with a request to recall sets of 6 digits played while they were composing. Both the presentation of the irrelevant speech (Salame & Baddeley, 1982) and of the digit load task (Baddeley & Hitch, 1974) had previously been shown to interfere with the ability of people to remember lists of materials presented for serial recall. Baddeley and Hitch (1974) also claimed that concurrent digit loads impeded performance in reasoning and comprehension tasks. Ransdell and Levy observed large and statistically reliable decrements in writers' fluency both when they encountered irrelevant speech during composition and when they were given the digit-recall task compared to when they wrote without these elements. However, only the recall task designed to tax the central executive resulted in a statistically significant decline in the quality of the essays. Moreover, the effects of the recall task on various measures of writing (such as the duration, frequency and location of pauses) were much more pervasive than the effects of the irrelevant speech, consistent with Baddeley's model.

Puzzled by the dissociation of writing fluency and quality when they presented irrelevant speech, Ransdell and Levy suggested that writers slow their rate of production in the presence of irrelevant speech in order to produce a coherent, quality text. Thus, their writers may have experienced difficulty in generating sentences, as predicted by the working memory model, but elected to slow down the rate of production to preserve the quality of output from the formulation and monitoring processes.

Brown, McDonald, Brown, and Carr (1988) claimed that the formulation system takes priority over execution in their work on handwriting of material read or re-called from memory. The Ransdell and Levy (1996a) experiments are the first to document a similar outcome for original composition. Their results suggested that writers allocate central executive capacity to maintain the quality of written text, despite secondary loads on it or on other components of working memory. This strategy fails only when insufficient central resources are available, as happens when six digits must be simultaneously remembered.

The experiments by Ransdell and Levy (1996a) represented initial attempts to determine if a plausible empirical case could be made for applying the Baddeley model to writing. They were not designed to enable *direct* tests of the contributions of working memory to the distinct writing processes that Kellogg (1996) described. In order to achieve this, a different paradigm was needed, one that would enable each of the subprocesses to be studied in isolation from the other. Lea and Levy elsewhere in this volume describe one approach to directly testing the contributions of phonological loop and the visuospatial sketchpad to the writing processes delin-eated in Kellogg's model. In this chapter, we describe another.

We attempted here to devise tasks that would carve up the very complex proc-ess of writing as neatly as possible into its constituents so that we could focus on each in isolation from the others. This approach is a very traditional one that psy-chologists have used to study a multitude of other complex processes, such as memory and text comprehension. We used the approach cautiously here, realizing that an activity as complex as text production may not be entirely understood in terms of the sum of the contributions of its individual components. Nevertheless, we believe that these experiments provide rather strong assessments of the basic claims of Kellogg's model.

Each of the first three experiments that we report was designed to tap only one of the processes identified in the model. We studied a group of 36 university stu-dents during periods in which they performed a task designed to tap only the ex-ecution process, for example, while an irrelevant message was spoken over their headphones. The same students also performed the same task in the absence of irrelevant speech. When given, the irrelevant speech consisted of one of several children's fables that was "read aloud" by a text-to-speech program, which ensured equal presentation characteristics.

Immediately before they began Experiments 1, 2, and 3, the students completed a self-paced tutorial that fully demonstrated the task, and gave them a few minutes practice before the experimental trials began. They were assigned equally often to each of the six possible sequences of the three experiments.

2   EXPERIMENT 1: THE EXECUTION PROCESS

To examine the execution process on its own, we presented writers with two large windows on their computer displays. One window contained several paragraphs of intrinsically interesting text. The other was initially blank, and formed a space into which the participants could copy, as quickly and as accurately as possible, the text that we displayed. We gave them 3 minutes to do this task, and measured their speed and accuracy.

Because, in Kellogg's model, the execution process has no direct link to the pho-nological loop, irrelevant speech should have no influence on writers during the copying task. As shown in Table 1, we found virtually identical performance by the writers who copied text in the presence and in the absence of irrelevant speech. For example, with irrelevant speech, the writers copied an average of 75.5 words and without it, they copied an average of 77.4 words. With the irrelevant speech, they made an average of 1.8 errors, and without it the result was 2.7 errors. These patterns and magnitude differences were not reliably altered when the observations were adjusted for the writers' typing speeds. There were indistinguishable differences between the very small number of false positives in the speech and no-speech conditions. None of these comparisons reflected reliable differences, just as the model predicts.

Table 1   *Means of performance measures in the execution process experiment. Standard errors in parentheses.*

	Non-speech condition	Speech condition
Mean number of words typed	77.4 (5.3)	75.5 (4.9)
Mean number of words typed correctly	74.7 (4.7)	73.7 (4.8)

3   EXPERIMENT 2: THE MONITORING PROCESS

The second experimental task was devised to engage the monitoring process independently of formulating and execution. Here, participants viewed one of two 240-word, 3-paragraph selections from *Psychology Today*. The passages were matched for number of sentences, sentence per paragraph, and words per sentence. The Flesch-Kincaid reading levels were 7.9 and 8.1. One passage was presented with and the other without irrelevant speech, counterbalanced across participants.

Each passage contained 5 spelling errors and 15 contextual errors. Contextual errors included inappropriate verb use, improper sentence structure (for example, a sentence fragment or a sentence ending with a preposition), improper use or omission of a comma or apostrophe, inappropriate pronoun, and improper word use (e.g., "farther" instead of "further"). The software enabled participants to highlight an error in the text and then to specify which of the different types of errors listed on the screen best characterized the mistake. As a result, we measured the percentage of contextual and spelling errors detected and correctly categorized, detected but not correctly identified, and false alarms.

According to Kellogg, the role of the phonological loop in monitoring is the result of the engagement of the reading subprocess, but not the editing subprocess. While our proofreading task certainly involved reading, the more demanding aspect of the task required identifying and classifying the errors that we had inserted into the paragraphs displayed. Thus, Kellogg's model predicts that involving the phonological loop with irrelevant speech should produce little or no influence on the monitoring task used here.

As reflected in Table 2, the results with and without irrelevant speech for the proofreading task were very similar. Overall, our participants detected a similar percentage of the errors in silence as they did during the irrelevant speech condition. Neither the percentage of the detections for the 15 non-spelling errors nor the

Table 2   *Means of performance measures in the monitoring process experiment. Standard*
          errors in parentheses.

	Non-speech	Speech
Mean percentage of errors detected	37.6 (2.8)	41.1 (2.4)
Mean percentage of spelling errors detected	32.2 (4.3)	38.3 (3.9)
Mean percentage of contextual errors detected	39.4 (3.1)	42.0 (2.4)

percentage of the 5 spelling errors differed significantly between the irrelevant speech conditions. For that matter, the rates for detecting the non-spelling errors were comparable to the rates for detecting the spelling errors. Most of the errors that were detected were also correctly identified but —as in the execution process experiment — the results were not different when the same people heard the irrelevant speech or did not hear it. This pattern of results is also consistent with Kellogg's model.

Thus far, we have seen that irrelevant speech does not seem to affect an individual's ability to perform either a task designed to tap only the execution component of writing or the editing component of monitoring, as anticipated by Kellogg's model. Because such null results could simply be a consequence of sloppy technique or insufficient statistical power, they would ordinarily be of much interest were it not for the fact that the irrelevant speech had noteworthy effects in the formulation experiment. Given the number of observations available for our comparisons, however, the experiments had more than ample statistical power to be able to correctly identify small differences as statistically reliable. Although we are not about to claim that we have proved a null hypothesis, the power analysis suggests that adding additional participants in effort to be able to reject the null hypothesis would not be a worthwhile endeavour.

4   EXPERIMENT 3: THE FORMULATING PROCESS

To study the formulating process independently of the monitoring and execution processes, participants were instructed to view a group of 5 words (e.g., ANGRILY, IMPACT, REACTED, CITIZENS, RECENT) until they had created a single sentence that used every word.

Each set of 5 words could be combined with other words and rearranged in many different ways to form a variety of grammatically correct sentences. Participants were cautioned to use the words in the form in which they were shown; that is, they were not to change singular words to plurals or to change past tense verbs to the present tense.

When the words first appeared on the computer display, a timer began to accumulate the number of milliseconds devoted to the formulation of the sentence. During this period, it was impossible for participants to enter text. The response latency was recorded when the participant clicked an on-screen button to indicate that he or she had completed formulating the sentence. When that occurred, the five words disappeared from the screen and a typing area was made available for the participant to enter the sentence that had been formulated.

This technique enables a reasonably pure estimate of the time that participants devote to formulating a sentence. Of course, they could click the mouse prematurely and continue to formulate, but this might result in an extended period before they entered their first word, which seldom occurred. The net effect, however, would be to underestimate rather than to overestimate the amount of time devoted to formulation.

Participants received 10 sets of five words to use in formulating their sentences in relative silence and another 10 sets of words, counterbalanced across participants, when they later repeated the task during the irrelevant speech condition.

Kellogg (1996) maintained that the formulating process places the heaviest demands on working memory because the visuospatial sketchpad, phonological loop, and the central executive may all be engaged. He theorized that the phonological loop was involved in the process of translating ideas into acceptable sentences when, for example, writers talk to themselves covertly [using their "inner voice" (Baddeley & Lewis, 1981)] as they generate sentences. Based on research using memory tasks (e.g., Salame & Baddeley, 1982) showing performance decrements when irrelevant speech messages are played during those tasks, we anticipated that irrelevant speech might similarly disrupt writing performance that depends heavily on memory. In Kellogg's conceptualization, this was most likely to occur during the moments that writers were attempting to formulate their sentences. Perhaps the disruptive effects of irrelevant speech reported by Ransdell and Levy (1996a) were the result of interference with the translating component of the formulating process. If this is correct, and if we can assume that our new paradigm focuses the writer's attention solely on the formulating process by preventing overt execution and monitoring processes, then writing performance should decline compared to the same activity during relative silence. In order to estimate how pervasive this effect was, we measured (a) the amount of time that writers took to formulate their sentences, (b) the time spent typing their sentences, (c) the number of target words used in the sentence in any form, (d) the number of target words used – as instructed – in the form originally displayed, and (e) the quality of the sentences produced.

Measuring the quality of a single sentence involves entirely different considerations than evaluating the quality of a paragraph or an essay. Very few of the dimensions used in the SSQS quality scoring system described by Ransdell and Levy (1996b) were appropriate or adaptable to single sentences. The sorting task used by Johnson, Linton, and Madigan (1994) also seemed to be inappropriate in this context. Accordingly, we created a simple 5-point quality scale that focused on meaningfulness and grammaticality, whose use is described later.

We measured several variables in the formulation experiment, including the time spent creating the sentences, the percentage of target words that were eventually incorporated into the sentences, and the quality of the sentences generated. The total time allotted to mentally creating sentences was similar for the two irrelevant speech conditions, averaging about 30 sec to formulate each sentence from the five displayed words. About 90% of the time, participants signaled that they had completed the task of mentally creating their sentences in less than the 45 sec we allowed, and this figure was not influenced by the presence of irrelevant speech.

In contrast, as reflected in Table 3, the percentage of stimulus words used in their exact form (for example, without changing singular words to plural forms) dropped significantly when writers had to deal with irrelevant speech, $F(1, 34) =$

Table 3   *Means of performance measures in the formulating process experiment. Stand-ard errors in parentheses.*

	Non-speech	Speech
Mean percentage of target words included in sentences (exact form)	81.8 (1.5)	74.5 (2.3)
Mean number of target words used	102 (3.9)	96 (4.1)
Mean quality	4.16 (0.11)	3.89 (0.14)

24.72, $p < .01$. This held true whether we used a lax or a strict criterion for counting hits. The strict criterion allowed a response to be included as a hit if the word appeared in a sentence in the same form as it was presented. In the lax criterion, any form of the word was acceptable.

To measure the quality of the sentences, raters independently classified each sentence into one of five categories, based on a combination of meaningfulness and grammaticality. The best possible sentence was one that was complete, meaningful, and free of grammatical errors. We did not penalize a response if it contained typographical errors, capitalization problems, or if it terminated without proper punctuation. The sentences were uniformly printed and presented to two judges who independently evaluated each item. Whenever these judges differed by more than one point in their judgment of a sentence, a third judge independently rescored it. This was necessary for about 6% of the 720 sentences. The overall correlation between the final quality scores of the judges was 0.86.

One of the important findings to come out of this study is that sentence quality declined significantly – about 6.5 % – when irrelevant speech was introduced into the task, $F(1, 34) = 5.54$, $p < .02$. This was the first time that we had found a reliable deterioration in writing quality when irrelevant speech was introduced into the experimental environment.

5   EXPERIMENT 4: A REPLICATION

To provide further support for this finding, we conducted a replication that was – with one exception – methodologically equivalent to the study just described. In addition to the irrelevant speech used previously, some writers heard the same words in a scrambled order. The speech was delivered in both cases by a text-to-speech computer program to ensure that the words in the scrambled condition would be delivered with the same inflections as those delivered in the natural word order. Twenty-four university students who had not participated in any of the previous studies formulated sentences using the original fables as irrelevant speech and 24 other experimentally naïve students heard the same words rearranged to form meaningless text. Thus, some of the writers might hear

THERE WAS ONCE A RICH AND WICKED OLD KING WHO HAD A LOVELY DAUGHTER

and others would hear

ONCE KING THERE A HAD WHO DAUGHTER OLD A RICH WAS AND WICKED LOVELY.

In both conditions, the writers must process exactly the same words on a sentence-by-sentence basis. If information in the phonological loop is continuously processed for meaning, then when the irrelevant speech is relatively more "natural" there should be greater burdens placed on working memory than when the speech consists of apparently unrelated words. This should result in longer formulating times. Moreover, if the burden is sufficiently great to involve the central executive, the more "natural" irrelevant speech should cause the writers to produce lower-quality sentences.

No such effects occurred. The two versions of irrelevant speech produced comparable decrements in sentence quality and virtually identical formulation times. This suggests that it is the phonemic, but probably not the syntactic or the semantic, information present in irrelevant speech that is processed – at least during the cognitively demanding text-formulating stage of writing. This suggestion that the locus of the irrelevant speech effect on planning and sentence generation may be phonological in nature is consistent with Kellogg's model.

6   CONTRASTING FINDINGS

These results contrast with those of Ransdell and Levy (1996a) that we referred to earlier. There, writers appeared to do all that they could to maintain quality when presented with tasks that loaded their phonological systems. In other words, there was comparatively little degradation in the quality of essays when irrelevant speech was introduced into the writing environment compared to the essays composed by the same writers in the absence of irrelevant speech. In contrast, we reported for the studies described in this chapter a small, but reliable, degradation in quality when exactly the same irrelevant messages were played while subjects formulated their sentences. The follow-up formulation study produced decrements in writing quality, independent of the meaningfulness of the message in the irrelevant speech.

There are substantial differences in the ways that we determined fluency and quality in these studies. Perhaps these differences in methodology ultimately will account for the differences in outcomes. We cannot help but wonder, however, if a meaningful part of the differences are due to the very different task demands placed on our writers. When a writer is asked to ignore irrelevant speech, to the extent that such speech is processed automatically and inevitably by a phonological system in working memory, there may be only minor disruptions to the writing process such as those that Ransdell and Levy (1996a) reported. In contrast, when writers must hold in memory more words than the phonological loop can deal with and simultaneously process irrelevant speech in the phonological loop at some level (as in the formulation studies reported here), it may not be unreasonable that some aspect of writing suffers. Baddeley (1986) maintained that the phonological loop can store only about 3 digits. Five unrelated words in working memory should therefore exceed its capacity. In this context, finding decrements in quality and in memory for the words presented while irrelevant speech is played is wholly consistent with Kellogg's writing model.

7   A RECONCILIATION

In an attempt to reconcile the apparently inconsistent findings between the Ransdell and Levy (1996a) studies and the experiments just described, we re-examined the essays and fluency data collected by Ransdell and Levy so as to approximate the conditions present here. The basis for this re-examination is as follows: Each single sentence that our writers crafted from the words provided to them resembles the initial sentence of a paragraph. Writers begin with information in working memory (from the words we presented) or from the topic presented (for the initial sentence of an essay) or the text previously composed (for the initial sentence of subsequent paragraphs). Unlike essay writing, where writers can continue generating text after completing an initial sentence, in the present formulation studies, they were never able to expand upon their ideas presented in any subsequent sentence. The crux of the reconciliation may then lie in the patterns of pauses that are exhibited. It has long been known that writers pause for longer durations between paragraphs than they do between sentences or between words. The conventional wisdom is that they are devoting this extra time to planning what to include in their next paragraph. (Of course, they could also be using a portion of this time re-reading what they have composed.) In Kellogg's model, we might anticipate that this additional time might also be devoted to the internal translation process. If so, then irrelevant speech, through its involvement with the phonological loop, might have its greatest effect when a writer is crafting the initial sentence of a paragraph.

The other discrepancy between the studies was associated with the role of irrelevant speech on writing quality scores. Because the amount of time spent formulating a *document* is weakly to moderately correlated with the overall quality of the document, it may be the case that a similar positive relationship exists between the amount of time spent formulating an individual *sentence* and its overall quality. We might thus expect the initial sentence of a paragraph – associated with greater formulation time – to be of higher quality than a representative sentence selected from elsewhere in the paragraph, which tends to be associated with a shorter pre-sentence pause duration and, presumably, shorter formulation time. Because an essay contains only one initial sentence per paragraph, and generally more than one additional sentence, the average quality of all the sentences in an essay will therefore tend to be lower than the average quality of the initial sentences. Finally, if much of the pause time preceding the execution of the initial sentence of a paragraph is the result of formulating processes that work as described in Kellogg's model, it would be reasonable to predict that irrelevant speech would have a greater deleterious effect on the quality of the initial sentence than subsequent sentences of a paragraph.

Accordingly, we focused on a comparison of the first sentence in each paragraph and one other arbitrarily selected sentence from the same paragraph in the essays composed by the writers in the Ransdell and Levy (1996a) study. The 310 sentences from the essays generated in the irrelevant speech condition and the no-speech condition were coded, randomized, then presented to eight judges who independently scored each sentence using the quality scale that we developed for evaluating the single sentences in the formulation studies. Using the same procedures, these judges also scored 330 comparable sentences generated by the writers in the Ransdell and Levy study who composed during the digit load and no digit load conditions. In addition, the FauxWord (Levy, 1994) data files, which contained each keystroke and the time it occurred during the composition sessions, provided

Table 4   *Means for the performance measures in the re-analyses of the Ransdell and Levy*
             (1996a) experiments. Standard errors in parentheses.

IRRELEVANT SPEECH EXPERIMENT	No irrelevant speech condition		Irrelevant speech condition	
	Initial sentences	*Other sentences*	*Initial sentences*	*Other sentences*
Mean quality	4.32 (0.11)	3.98 (0.14)	4.32 (0.08)	4.06 (0.10)
Mean fluency (words per minute excluding between-word pauses)	36.21 (2.15)	38.75 (2.39)	33.04 (1.57)	35.67 (2.21)
Mean pause times between words (sec)	0.79 (0.14)	0.85 (0.14)	1.14 (0.01)	0.98 (0.01)
Mean pause times before sentence (sec)	11.99 (0.50)	6.34 (0.22)	19.14 (0.31)	5.51 (0.12)

DIGIT LOAD EXPERIMENT	No digit load condition		Digit load condition	
	Initial sentences	*Other sentences*	*Initial sentences*	*Other sentences*
Mean quality	4.55 (0.10)	4.16 (0.10)	4.42 (0.11)	4.09 (0.11)
Mean fluency (words per minute excluding between-word pauses)	34.10 (1.35)	34.87 (1.67)	25.42 (1.41)	25.40 (1.46)
Mean pause times between words (sec)	0.86 (0.06)	0.86 (0.06)	1.85 (0.15)	1.79 (0.15)
Mean pause times before sentence (sec)	6.63 (0.96)	3.98 (0.48)	14.69 (3.61)	10.97 (2.09)

information that enabled us to make a number of pause-based comparisons that had not been done in the original study. The results of these re-analyses appear in Table 4.

Analyses of variance indicated that the initial sentence of paragraphs was judged higher in quality than a randomly selected other sentence within the same paragraph, $F(1, 327) = 7.69$, $p < .006$. If the quality of a single sentence could be assessed in the same way that an entire essay can be evaluated holistically, it would be tempting to suggest that this difference might be due to the ease with which the sentences could be interpreted. The first sentence of a paragraph will often be interpretable with less contextual information than one in the middle of a paragraph, which could lead to its receiving a higher quality rating. As noted earlier, however, the assessment of the quality of single sentences was based on their grammaticality and well-formedness, rendering this interpretation moot. The same analysis of variance indicated that there was no reduction in sentence quality when writers composed while presented with irrelevant speech to ignore relative to no-speech control conditions.

The configuration of the results changed markedly when analysing of fluency and pauses. A relatively pure measure of writing fluency (words per minute typed, excluding the time spent pausing between words) indicated that irrelevant speech reliably slowed writers down by about 8%. This percentage decline is somewhat less than that reported by Ransdell and Levy, but their measure of fluency included pause times between words, sentences and paragraphs. A measure of planning time, involving the lengths of the pauses immediately before the critical sentences, showed that writers spent over 160% more time pausing prior to crafting the initial sentences of their paragraphs than they did for sentences within those paragraphs.

This significant difference (p < .001) depended, however, upon the writing condition: when irrelevant speech was being presented, planning time was 247% longer for initial sentences, but during the comparison periods without irrelevant speech, it was only 89% longer for these sentences.

The analyses of the quality of sentences generated during the digit load and no digit load conditions in Ransdell and Levy (1996a) also paralleled those in the original report (i.e., digit load depressed quality), but the outcome was only marginally significant. Similar to the results obtained in the analysis of the irrelevant speech study, the initial sentences of paragraphs were of higher quality than other, comparison sentences, F(1, 352) = 14.88, p < .001. In none of the analyses of quality was there an interaction between type of sentence (initial vs. other) and type of ancillary task presented during writing.

Recall that in the formulation studies described earlier, writing quality suffered when irrelevant speech was presented. In the Ransdell and Levy (1996a) data, as originally analysed, essay quality was affected by the digit load task, but not by irrelevant speech. The pattern of results obtained in our re-analysis of the Ransdell and Levy data was unchanged when we focused only on individual sentences and used the very different quality scoring scale that we developed for the formulation studies. Although the quality of the initial sentences was greater than those that followed in a paragraph, the lack of a main effect for irrelevant speech and the failure to find a significant interaction between the two independent variables parallels exactly the original findings reported by Ransdell and Levy. Moreover, the reanalysis of the digit load study after deploying the new scoring scale on the individual sentences was consistent with the findings of the original study.

Thus, it seems clear that although the differences in pre-sentence pause times that occur before initial and subsequent sentences of a paragraph are related to differences in the quality of those sentences, the effect of irrelevant speech was generally small across the sentences of a paragraph. This pattern of results is consistent with a model, such as Kellogg's, that relegates only a portion of sentence formulation time to regulation by a phonological loop. These data suggest that such regulation is minimal if most of the time that might be attributed to a combination of planning and translating is devoted to planning. In Kellogg's model, the phonological loop plays no role in planning.

Nevertheless, there remains the task of explaining, in the original data reported here for the formulation studies, why sentence quality was disrupted by irrelevant speech. The answer cannot lie in the new quality scoring scale, because when that scale was used in the re-analysis of the individual sentences in the Ransdell and Levy study, the outcome did not change. The answer cannot lie in the attention value of the irrelevant speech, because both series of studies used the same children's fables. We have identified, however, two plausible explanations.

First, as Kellogg (1997) has noted, it is possible that the demand characteristics of the writing task influence the manner in which writers cope with the distractions. In the essay and paragraph tasks, writers may interpret their primary goal to be the production of a quality text. In contrast, in the sentence production task, they might interpret their goal to be rapid output, and this might result in a reduction in the quality of their text. Without a replication of both studies that would include an index of the writers' perceptions of their goals, this potential explanation can be neither supported nor rejected.

An alternative explanation is based on a different consideration of task demands. It may be that burdening writers with the importance of remembering five unrelated words while they rearrange them and add appropriate connectives to form a complete sentence may load working memory as heavily as asking writers to remember six digits while they generate their own texts. In both of those situations, writing quality suffered relative to control conditions. These considerations led to the final study that we will address next.

8   EXPERIMENT 5

We modified the procedure used in our formulation process studies so that writers were given only a topic title (for example, "The Perfect Job") to process rather than a series of words. Timing began at the moment the topic title was displayed. Of special interest was the time between that moment and when the writer began writing the first sentence. This time should include only the planning and/or translating components of the formulation process. Working memory would clearly be engaged, primarily by writers accessing appropriate content from long-term memory and their efforts to coherently arrange that content. Writers would not be additionally burdened by the need to retain unrelated words in working memory during this interval.

A new group of undergraduate volunteers (N = 24) was given as much time as they wished to perform the task, but each trial of the experiment actually ended when the writer pressed the Enter key to initiate a second paragraph. Participants wrote paragraphs on two topics, with and without irrelevant speech, in a counterbalanced ABBA or BAAB order. The topics were those used by Levy and Ransdell (1995) and by Ransdell and Levy (1996a). The materials used for the irrelevant speech were the same fables as used in the previous studies. On average, the paragraphs contained about 211 words and were written over a period of about 10 minutes.

Two experienced judges, who were blind as to the writing condition, used the SSQS tool (Ransdell & Levy, 1996b) to independently evaluate each paragraph. The initial sentence and one other randomly selected sentence from the paragraph were extracted, randomly sequenced with the corresponding sentences generated by other writers, and assessed by the same two judges who were blind both to the writing condition and to the location of the sentence within the paragraph. They used the 5-point grammaticality-based scale described earlier to evaluate the quality of the individual sentences.

The time between the presentation of the title and the writers' first keystroke was used as the estimate of formulation time for the initial sentence. The estimate of the formulation time for the other sentence selected from the paragraph was the time between the occurrence of the final character of the preceding sentence and the keystroke beginning the sentence of interest. This estimate could be an overestimate if participants engaged in re-reading times or an underestimate if they began formulating a sentence while executing another. Writing fluency was calculated as the number of words typed per minute, excluding pause times between sentences because those times were used in the other, independent analyses.

Quality scores based on the sentence-by-sentence analysis, using the Marek-Levy scoring instrument, yielded the results that corresponded with those reported in our re-analysis of the data from Ransdell and Levy (1996a). That is, the initial sentence of a paragraph was again of higher quality (4.45) than a control sentence that followed it (3.89), F(1, 23) = 10.89, p <.001, whether the writing occurred during irrelevant speech or not. More importantly, irrelevant speech again produced only small, but statistically unreliable differences in sentence quality. Exactly the same pattern emerged when the scores on the more complex SSQS, involving assessments of the entire paragraph, were studied.

Similar correspondences between the studies occurred in the analyses of writing fluency. That is, overall words per minute, exclusive of pause times between words, were about 11% less when irrelevant speech was present than when it was not, F(1, 23) = 7.04, p <.001. This fluency decrement was nearly 10% greater for the initial than the subsequent sentences in a paragraph, F(1, 23) = 9.04, p < .001.

Estimates of formulation times (collected by measuring the interval between the presentation of the title of the essay and the writer's first keystroke) address claims made by Kellogg's model. When irrelevant speech was presented, this estimate of formulation time was 14% greater than for the comparable phase of writing without the irrelevant speech, F(1, 23) = 22.95, p <.001.

9   DISCUSSION AND CONCLUSIONS

Our goals at the outset of this chapter were to extend the findings reported by Ransdell and Levy (1996) that provided initial support for Kellogg's (1996) multicomponent model of writing. The five experiments reported here provide substantial data that, in the main, are consistent with the claims that this model makes about the role a construct such as a phonological loop has in the production of text. The first two experiments showed that irrelevant speech had no effect when presented while writers were doing tasks that focused on the executing or monitoring components of writing. In contrast, the third experiment showed that during a task requiring writers to focus on the formulating component of text production, their writing quality suffered in the presence of irrelevant speech. The fourth experiment demonstrated that the deleterious effects of irrelevant speech on text formulation did not depend upon there being any inherent meaning in the irrelevant stimulus. The final experiment examined the formulation process by focusing on the time between the presentation of the topic for an essay and the writer's first keystroke; the data showed a reliable increment of this time in the presence of irrelevant speech. The pattern emerging in the data from these studies generally supports the predictions about the involvement of the phonological loop in writing that are made or implied by Kellogg's model of writing. Lea and Levy (elsewhere in this volume) describe studies that focus on claims of this model about the involvement of the visuospatial sketchpad in text production. We note, however, that some of our findings are not clearly explained by this model.

Were our first formulation process experiments anomalies? After all, only there did irrelevant speech produce robust and negative effects on writing quality. We believe that those results are entirely compatible with the other data we have discussed. They may simply be the consequence of burdening writers with the task of remembering a set of unrelated words while simultaneously attempting to use them in their original form to create a meaningful and grammatically correct sentence. The original task may have placed burdens on working memory equivalent to those in the Ransdell and Levy (1996a) experiment requiring writers to keep six digits in memory, which also produced reductions in writing quality.

Our final experiment, which produced a more "natural" writing environment compared with that used in the first formulation studies, loaded working memory only with whatever information the writer accessed in long-term memory. (We assume that the topic of the essay itself did not load memory because, once revealed, it was continuously visible to the writer.) Such loading is highly variable and, to the best of our knowledge, not quantifiable with currently available tools. Nevertheless, whether the data were analyzed in a holistic manner, as Ransdell and Levy (1996a) did, or in a more molecular way, as we did in the formulation studies, we found consistent evidence of disruptions in the fluency with which writers composed when they were exposed to irrelevant speech. We also found that irrelevant speech affected writers differentially, depending upon whether they were generating the first or a subsequent sentence in a paragraph. This suggests that some parts of a composition place greater demands on the formulation process, something not obvious from Kellogg's model. An alternate explanation is that irrelevant speech affects both the translating and planning aspects of formulation, which is inconsistent with Kellogg's model.

Regardless, writers seem to use their available resources in a flexible way, allocating them differentially as they work on different portions of their documents. When composing in a highly artificial environment, such as the memory-intensive formulation task described earlier, writers seemed to work hard to craft sentences that included as many words as possible. Imposing a load on working memory by presenting irrelevant speech did not deter them from meeting this objective. What the additional load seemed to do, however, was to lessen their ability to form well-crafted sentences. The quality scale used to evaluate individual sentences focused mainly on how well-formed and complex the sentence was. Sophisticated clause structures, which were well within the writing repertoires of these university students, rarely appeared in their sentences in this composing environment.

In contrast, when composing "naturally" – that is, when the task constraints have a close resemblance to those with which the writer is familiar (such as writing short essays under variable and uncontrollable acoustic backgrounds that may include the sounds of other people talking) – adult writers seem to do whatever is necessary to preserve the quality of their work. This is true both at the sentence level and at the document level. Perhaps this is because this is what they believe we expect of them. Writers' goals, their understanding of audience expectations, and hypotheses about the researchers' objectives no doubt play an important role in formulating writers' strategies. Their interplay with working memory, poorly understood at present, represents a research challenge that warrants attention by those with interests in both the theoretical and the applied aspects of writing.

AUTHOR NOTE

We are greatly indebted to David Pollack and Courtney Smith for their able assistance in many of the analyses. We also appreciate the constructive comments provided by Ronald Kellogg and Lucile Chanquoy on earlier versions of this chapter. Correspondence concerning this chapter can be directed to C. Michael Levy, PhD., Department of Psychology, University of Florida, Box 112250, Gainesville, FL, USA 32611-2250 or by email to levy@ufl.edu.

REFERENCES

Atkinson, R. C., & Shriffrin, R. M. (1968) Human memory: A proposed system and its control processes. In K. W. Spence (Ed.), *The psychology of learning and motivation*. NY: Academic Press.

Baddeley, A. D. (1986). *Working memory*. Oxford: Oxford University Press.

Baddeley, A. D., & Hitch, G. J. (1974). Working memory. In G. Bower (Ed.), *The psychology of learning and motivation* (Vol. 8, pp. 47-90). NY: Academic Press.

Baddeley, A. D., & Lewis, V. J. (1981). Inner active processes in reading: The inner voice, the inner ear, and the inner eye. In A. M. Lesgold & C. A. Perfetti (Eds.), *Interactive processes and reading*, pp. 107-129. Hillsdale, NJ: Erlbaum.

Baddeley, A. D., Thomson, N., & Buchanan, M. (1975). Word length and the structure of short-term memory. *Journal of Verbal Learning and Verbal Behavior, 14*, 575-559.

Brown, J. S., McDonald, J. L., Brown, T. L., & Carr, T. H. (1988). Adapting to processing demands in discourse production: The case of handwriting. *Journal of Experimental Psychology: Human Perception and Performance, 14*, 45-59.

Colle, H. A., & Welsh, A. (1976). Acoustic masking and primary memory. *Journal of Verbal Learning and Verbal Behavior, 15*, 17-31.

Gathercole, S. E., & Baddeley, A. D. (1993). *Working memory and language*. London: Erlbaum.

Glenberg, A. M., & Swanson, N. G. (1986). A temporal distinctiveness theory of recency and modality effects. *Journal of Experimental Psychology: Learning, Memory, and Cognition, 12*, 3-15.

Grabowski, J. (1996). Writing and speaking: Common grounds and differences toward a regulation theory of written language production. In C. M. Levy & S. E. Ransdell (Eds.). *The science of writing* (pp 73-91). Mahwah, NJ: Erlbaum.

Hayes, J. R. (1996). A framework for understanding cognition and affect in writing. In C. M. Levy & S. E. Ransdell (Eds.). *The science of writing* (pp 1-27). Mahwah, NJ: Erlbaum.

Johnson, S. E., Linton, P. W., & Madigan, R. J. (1994). The role of internal standards in assessment of written discourse. *Discourse Processes, 18*, 231-245.

Jones, D. M. (1995). The fate of the unattended stimulus: Irrelevant speech and cognition. *Applied Cognitive Psychology, 9*, 523-538.

Kellogg, R. T. (1996). A model of working memory in writing. In C. M. Levy & S. E. Ransdell (Eds.). *The science of writing* (pp 57-71). Mahwah, NJ: Erlbaum.

Kellogg, R. T. (1997). Personal communication.

Levy, C. M. (1994). FauxWord and FastFauxWord: Windows-based tools for capturing and analyzing the process of written composition. In H. van den Bergh, T. van der Geest, D. Janssen, G. Rijlaarsdam, & S. Sengers (Eds.), *EARLI/ECWC 1994 Writing Conference abstracts*. Utrecht: Utrecht University Press.

Levy, C. M., & Ransdell, S. E. (1995). Is writing as difficult as it seems? *Memory & Cognition, 26*, 219-223.

LeCompte, D C. (1996). Irrelevant speech, serial rehearsal, and temporal distinctiveness: A new approach to the irrelevant speech effect. *Journal of Experimental Psychology: Learning, Memory, and Cognition, 22*, 1154-1165.

Madigan, R. J., Johnson, S. E., & Linton, P.W. (1994, June). Working memory capacity and the writing process. Paper presented at the American Psychological Society, Washington, D.C.

Ransdell, S. E., & Levy, C. M. (1996a). The effects of attended and unattended irrelevant speech and concurrent digit load on writing quality and fluency. Paper presented at the European Computers and Writing Conference, Barcelona.

Ransdell, S. E., & Levy, C. M. (1996b). Working memory constraints on writing quality and fluency. In C. M. Levy & S. E. Ransdell (Eds.). *The science of writing* (pp 93-106). Mahwah, NJ: Erlbaum.

Salame, P., & Baddeley, A. D. (1982). Disruption of short-term memory by unattended speech: Implications for the structure of working memory. *Journal of Verbal Learning and Verbal Behavior, 21*, 150-164.

Components of Working Memory in Text Production

Ronald T. Kellogg
University of Missouri, USA

ABSTRACT

Models of working memory vary in their treatment of capacity limitations, the number of components they posit, and other factors. This chapter considers the implications of the working memory literature for understanding how writers use their knowledge in solving the content and rhetorical problems of a composition task. Three hypotheses are posed and some of the relevant evidence reviewed. First, the most important constraint of working memory on writing skill is the limited capacity of the central executive. Second, transient working memory is not unitary and a complex task such as writing is likely to engage at least a verbal (phonological) component and a visual/spatial component that are separate from the central executive. Third, a non-transient component of working memory may also be used by writers with a high degree of domain-specific knowledge. Reliable access to long-term memory may lessen the capacity limitations of the central executive for such writers.

1   COMPONENTS OF WORKING MEMORY IN TEXT PRODUCTION

What a writer knows about the content and discourse structure of a text under production certainly matters. There is ample evidence that the nature of the resulting text is affected by the availability of relevant knowledge in long-term memory (e.g., Jeffery & Underwood, 1996; McCutchen, 1986; Nystrand, 1982; Stein, 1986; Schoonen & De Glopper, 1996; Wright & Rosenberg, 1993). But for knowledge to improve the product or guide the process, the writer must retrieve and apply the relevant procedures, schemas, facts, and episodes through the use of working memory (Kellogg, 1994). Without effective systems for reliably gaining access to knowledge, processing it in the context of the task at hand, and storing intermediate mental products, knowledge is inert. The present chapter examines the nature of the systems of working memory that enable writers to use what they know.

One approach to accounting for how working memory functions in writing tasks is the application of Baddeley's (1986) influential model, as described in Kellogg (1996). Working memory, according to Baddeley and his colleagues, includes a central executive that coordinates cognitive operations through scheduling and other attentional control. Two additional working memory components are the phonological loop and the visuo-spatial sketchpad. These store and maintain specific representational codes through rehearsal. The phonological loop stores and rehearses verbal information, whereas the sketchpad handles visual and spatial information.

The Baddeley model has many competitors, however. The simplest alternative portrays working memory as a single, central pool of resources and many theorists have adopted this as a sensible starting point in understanding both text comprehension (Engle, Cantor, & Carullo, 1992) and text production (McCutchen, 1996). Another alternative discounts the relevance of capacity limitations altogether by suggesting that experts draw on long-term memory in performing a task within their domain of specialized knowledge (Ericsson & Kintsch, 1995). It broadens the concept of working memory to include both short-term and long-term components. Others have assumed that working memory is transient and capacity limited, but have posited multiple capacities dedicated to verbal versus spatial processing (Shah & Miyake, 1996) or phonological versus semantic processing (Martin, Shelton, & Yaffee, 1994). Jonides and Smith (1997) integrated the multiple capacity approach with Baddeley's central executive. They documented that verbal, visual, and spatial working memory components are three separate systems, both functionally and anatomically, and suggested a fourth semantic component that stores and maintains propositional rather than perceptual codes. While Jonides and Smith retained the central executive, they broke it down into a set of executive functions. Examples of these include selective focusing of attention, inhibiting alternative focuses, planning responses, scheduling responses, and monitoring for errors.

In light of these many alternative conceptions, how should the role of working memory in writing be portrayed? The present chapter focuses on three hypotheses bearing on this question. First, the most important constraint of working memory on writing skill is the limited capacity of the central executive. It is assumed that individuals differ in attention, planning, monitoring and other executive functions and that any single individual experiences capacity limits in conducting these functions simultaneously. Because these executive functions are so integral to writing, the limited capacity of the executive component of working memory stands out as the chief constraint on using available knowledge. Multiple capacity models of working memory that exclude an important role for a central executive system of processes miss a key attribute of thinking and language use. Arguments that the capacity limitations of transient working memory are circumvented by long-term memory also risk missing this basic constraint.

Second, transient working memory is not unitary and a complex task such as writing likely engages all of its components. Transient working memory probably includes but is not limited to spatial, verbal, and central executive components. For example, spatial information may be processed by one component of the short-term system of working memory, whereas verbal information is processed by another. It is hypothesized that particular writing processes make unique demands on the code-specific components of working memory. If that is so, then it should be possible to disrupt writing performance in selective ways.

Third, a novel, non-transient component of working memory may come in the form of reliable access to domain-specific knowledge stored in long-term memory. A full account of how expert writers retrieve and use extensive knowledge about their topic perhaps needs to consider the hypothesis of long-term working memory. For experts in a domain, ready access to such long-term storage may lessen the capacity limits of the traditional short-term systems of working memory. In other words, the working memory system brought to bear in complex tasks such as writing and reading might include both the traditional short-term component or ST-WM and a long-term component or LT-WM for experts in a particular domain. Ericsson and Kintsch (1995) proposed LT-WM to explain reading without recourse to capacity limitations of working memory. Here it is suggested that even expert writers in a domain must still struggle with the capacity limitations of the transient components of working memory.

The chapter begins by briefly reviewing the assumptions of the Kellogg (1996) model of transient working memory in text production. Next, each of the three hypotheses is evaluated.

2 TRANSIENT WORKING MEMORY IN WRITING

2.1 Writing Processes

My earlier model linked work on the microstructure of language investigated in speech production and the macrostructure typically explored in writing research (Fayol, 1991). So, for example, the subprocesses required in the programming and execution of handwriting and the phonological, lexical, semantic, and grammatical subprocesses of sentence generation parallel the language production models of Garrett (1980), Bock (1982; 1995), Levelt (1989), and Bock and Levelt (1994). The idea generation, organization, and goal setting subprocesses of planning borrow from the Hayes and Flower (1980) model of text formulation. The model assumes three systems of production: The formulation of ideas and linguistic expression, motor execution, and monitoring of both formulation and execution processes. Each system involves two basic processes and numerous subprocesses. The *planning* of ideas and their *translation* into sentences are formulation processes; *programming* motor units and *executing* muscle movements are execution processes; *reading* already produced text and *editing* all mental and textual representation output from the formulation and execution systems are monitoring processes.

The dynamics of the three systems are as follows. The formulation system plans the content of a text and translates it into sentences. The execution system programs the motor output for handwriting, typing, or dictation. The monitoring system oversees the formulation and execution systems, detecting errors and signaling feedback for corrective operations. It receives both the output of the execution system, through reading already generated text, and output of the formulation system, through covert editing of the planning and translation processes. The writer may covertly edit thoughts and linguistic expressions under construction prior to their execution.

Editing here means flagging errors in the output of planning, translating, programming, and execution and signaling feedback to the appropriate process. Renewed activation of planning, translating, programming, and execution would then correct the error. Thus, the same process that generates ideas or sentences is responsible for generating corrections. Editing itself is concerned with signaling the need for corrections. Reading, editing, and error correction through renewed planning, translating, or programming can occur immediately after production of the error, but may also be delayed. The strategy adopted by the writer for allocating working memory to monitoring versus formulation and execution affects these matters of timing.

2.2 Demands on Working Memory

Five of the six basic processes make specific demands on the central executive, verbal or phonological, and visual/spatial components of working memory (Kellogg, 1996). These are summarized in Table 1. Only the execution of programmed muscle movements proceed fully automatically without any demands on working memory. However, the programming demands on the central executive are as-

Table 1   *The Components of Working Memory Used by the Six Basic Processes of Writing.*

Basic Process	Working memory component		
	Spatial	Central Executive	Verbal
Planning	X	X	
Translating		X	X
Programming		X[1]	
Executing			
Reading		X	X
Editing	X		

[1]For highly practiced motor skills, these demands are small if not negligible.

sumed to be small if not negligible when typing or handwriting skills are highly practiced. Planning, translating, reading, and editing may also vary from task to task in that the degree of their demands on the central executive may depend on past experience with the particular task. Even so, these four processes generally make significant demands on executive capacity according to the model and the available evidence supports this claim as will be documented in the next section.

The model allows the simultaneous activation of formulation, execution, and monitoring, as long as the demands placed on the central executive do not exceed its limited capacity. The model further assumes that the execution of a word or phrase may take place simultaneously with the formulation of new material or monitoring of already written material. This is possible only because execution can, when well-practiced, proceed virtually automatically. The basic processes of formulation and monitoring, on the other hand, are in many respects controlled and effortful.

Formulation
Planning demands the visual/spatial and the executive components of working memory. When writers plan by visualizing ideas, organizational schemes, supporting graphics, appearances of the orthography and layout, then they engage the visual/spatial components. Creating ideas (Shepard, 1978) and recalling them from long-term memory (Paivio, 1986) can invoke visual imagery. The visual working memory system is used in object recognition to inform about what is perceived in the environment (Jonides & Smith, 1997). Conceivably, writers draw on the same system in imagining visually coded ideas. For example, in composing definitions of concrete words, adults reported using imagery more often than in defining abstract words. They also began sooner and wrote better definitions for the concrete than the abstract words (Sadowski, Kealy, Goetz, & Paivio, 1997). It is plausible that the visual working memory system is involved in processing and using knowledge about concrete words to write their definitions. Drawing network diagrams and other organizational devices probably draws on the spatial component of working memory. Outlining, for example, significantly improves the quality of the resulting text (Kellogg, 1988; Rau & Sebrechts, 1996); presumably the spatial component is at work in helping writers to organize their ideas hierarchically.

Given that planning any action is a key executive function (Shallice & Burgess, 1991; Gathercole & Baddeley, 1993; Jonides & Smith, 1997), it is natural to assign the central executive to the planning of texts. Generating ideas, trying out various organizational schemes, and establishing an appropriate tone all entail high levels of reflective thought and metacognitive awareness (Flower & Hayes, 1980; Hayes, 1996). Planning, along with monitoring, underlies the self-regulatory aspects of writing that are so closely aligned with executive functions. Writers must intentionally initiate and sustain their work through countless distractions (Graham & Harris, 1997; Zimmerman & Risemberg, 1997).

Translating an idea into a sentence first involves a grammatical component featuring functional and positional processing and then a phonological component (Bock & Levelt, 1994; Bock, 1995). The phonological representations of the sentence constituents are temporarily processed and stored in verbal working memory, according to the present model. Further, the writer may rehearse or maintain these representations in verbal working memory for covert editing. Alternatively, the representations may be processed and output for immediate execution, as happens when writers type sentences seemingly as fast as they think of them.

In addition to the verbal component, translating at times demands the central executive. Although sentence generation is largely automatic in conversational speech, the effort required varies with the situation (Bock, 1982). In text production, translation appears to be effortful judging from secondary task measurements (Kellogg, 1994). When a writer must struggle to find just the right words and sentence structures, the demands on the central executive can be significant. An interesting experimental demonstration of the executive demands of translation was reported by Fayol, Largy, and Lemaire (1994). When required to retain five words while simultaneously transcribing orally presented sentences, writers make subject-verb agreement errors in French. Specifically, the writers incorrectly inflected the verb to a plural form if an object of a preposition closest to the verb was plural and the more remote subject noun was singular. If one accepts that retaining five words places a demand on the central executive as well as verbal working memory, then these results convincingly show a role for executive functions in grammatical processing.

Execution and Monitoring
Handwriting, typing or dictating presumably make demands only on the central executive and these are minimal when the skills are well-practiced. For a novice, the demands of behavioral output can be substantial. Novel activities of all kinds require the central executive to control the schemas used in motor output. For example, handwriting demands more attention than speaking in young children, but both modes of output demand little attention by early adulthood (Bourdin & Fayol, 1994). It is the programming, not the executing, of muscle movements that demands the central executive in the present model.

The editing process demands only the central executive, but unlike programming, error detection presumably requires substantial capacity even in highly skilled writers. The reason is that there are so many ways to make mistakes. Editing must take place at all of the many levels of text structure, from the detection of an error in motor programming to a problem in the organization of ideas in a text. The monitoring of errors along with the planning of actions are key executive functions.

Any error detection at any level of text production thus adds to the burden of the central executive according to this view.

Editing sometimes occurs covertly prior to handwriting or typing the formulated sentence(s). It may also occur at any time after execution. If there is sufficient delay between the formulation of a sentence and editing, the writer must first read the already produced text in order to engage in editing. The reading process itself is known to be highly complex and demanding of working memory (Just & Carpenter, 1992). With respect to the model, reading places demands on both the verbal component and the executive component (Gathercole & Baddeley, 1993).

As a point of clarification, the term revision refers to much more than the reading and editing processes of the monitoring system. Fitzgerald (1987; p. 484) explained that revision "involves identifying discrepancies between intended and instantiated text, deciding what could or should be changed in the text and how to make the desired changes, and . . . making the desired changes." In revision, as in the original drafting of text, the writer engages in all the processes of formulation and execution as well as monitoring. Editing and reading then are only two aspects of the revision of previously written texts. The correction of errors thus invokes the same processes that generated them in the first place. Only the detection of a mistake or discrepancy is assigned to the executive function of editing, which then signals feedback to the formulation or execution systems as needed.

To summarize, formulation and monitoring place greater demands on working memory than execution, unless the mode of output is unskilled. The functions of the executive component of working memory are vital to all aspects of text production, except moving the muscles themselves.

3   EVIDENCE ON THE THREE HYPOTHESES

Evidence on the three hypotheses about the role of working memory in the production of written texts is considered next. The first two concern aspects of transient working memory that are consistent with the Kellogg (1996) model discussed above. The third raises an aspect that falls outside the scope of any model that limits working memory to short-term processing and storage.

3.1 Central Executive Limitations

The view that people are limited in their ability to perform multiple tasks simultaneously has a distinguished pedigree. Cowan (1995) provided a contemporary defense of the proposition that central attentional limits must be included in any viable model of human information processing. His theme of limited central attention abilities echoed Broadbent's (1958) and Kahneman's (1973) classic treatises on the subject. In the development of writing skill, McCutchen (1986) has offered compelling evidence of the importance of a limited capacity system of working memory. Further, the classic Hayes and Flower (1980) model of adult writers stressed the point that demands can readily overload attentional capacity.

The proposed model assumes that planning, translating, reading, and editing generally make significant demands on the central executive, and programming may add to this demand in executing non-routine output. The quality and timing of their outputs depends on the degree to which they gain access to the functions of a central executive of limited capacity. These processes are thus resource limited (Norman & Bobrow, 1975).

Several studies have clearly documented the point that writing often makes heavy demands on working memory. Kellogg (1994) reported comparisons in these demands among planning, translating, and reviewing (reading and editing combined) in writing with incidental learning, intentional learning, reading syntactically simple versus complex text, and playing chess.

Working memory demands were measured using secondary probe reaction time to an auditory signal presented during the primary task. In the writing task, a key was pressed after orally responding to the signal to indicate whether the writer was planning, translating, or reviewing at the time of the interruption. The more interference (compared with baseline measurements) in probe RT while engaged in, say, planning a text, the more momentary cognitive effort the writer is devoting to the task. Presumably, the executive functions of focusing attention on the detection of the tone and scheduling a response to it are slowed when they are deeply engaged in the writing task. The results showed that planning and reviewing in particular caused the most RT interference, but even translating was highly effortful, with detection times slowing about 350 ms over baseline times collected in a simple RT task. All the learning and reading tasks showed interference below 200 ms. Only chess playing was comparable to the writing task in its working memory demands. Comparable high levels of interference in writing tasks have been reported by Piolat, Roussey, Olive, and Farioli (1996; Piolat, 1998).

Not only do multiple basic processes all depend on the central executive, each process entails diverse and demanding subprocesses. The thinking processes involved in generating ideas in verbal or imaginal formats, spatially organizing ideas, and anticipating the reader's expectations illustrate the diversity of planning demands alone. If several basic processes and their constituent subprocesses all draw on the central executive, then one would expect trade-offs within a system and even across the formulation, execution, and monitoring systems. Also, individual differences in central executive capacity should correlate with writing ability. Studies on these points are discussed next.

Trade-offs

In the developmental and learning disabilities literature, some evidence indicates that struggling with mechanical demands, such as correct spelling, disrupts planning ideas (Graham, 1990; Graham, Beringer, Abbott, Abbott, & Whitaker, 1997). This illustrates a trade-off between attending to planning versus the subprocesses of translation involved in written spelling. Difficulties with handwriting or typing may also disrupt the planning of content, illustrating a trade-off between the formulation and execution systems. Graham et al. found that writing fluency was related significantly to both spelling and handwriting in first, second, and third grade children. For fourth, fifth, and sixth graders, spelling had been sufficiently mastered so that it no longer affected fluency. The quality of writing was reliably related to only handwriting for all the age groups studied. Furthermore, the use of dictation eliminates the mechanical demands of spelling and handwriting. When fourth and sixth graders of average writing ability dictate their texts, fluency improves resulting in longer compositions but the quality does not change (Scardamalia & Bereiter, 1986). For poor writers, however, both quality and fluency gains have been observed through the use of dictation (Graham, 1990).

Bourdin and Fayol (1994; 1996) convincingly demonstrated trade-offs between the formulation and execution systems in several experiments (Fayol, this volume). They found a Mode (oral versus written) by Age interaction effect in the short-term retention of words and in language production. The low-level aspects of graphic transcription and spelling are not automatized in young children and these processes draw working memory resources away from high-level processes. Young children remember fewer words in a serial recall task when they produce them in writing than when they do so orally. This difference is not observed in adults, for whom the execution processes of writing demand little if any central executive capacity. The recall task can be viewed as a simplified language production task in which the lexical items held in verbal working memory are already formulated and simply require execution. Bourdin and Fayol (1996) found the same trade-off for young children in sentence production. They compared a speaking versus writing span test that combined sentence production with the storage and recall of words. Children, but not adults, showed a higher speaking span than writing span. Their results, then, clearly demonstrate that the formulation and execution systems share a common component of working memory in children.

Similar trade-offs occur in adult writers, too, in different circumstances. Glynn, Britton, Muth, and Dogan (1982) examined the number of arguments generated by students in a persuasive writing task. Instructions in the unordered-proposition condition encouraged the writers to focus exclusively on generating ideas. The ordered propositions condition prompted them to generate and organize their ideas, but not to worry about the manner in which they expressed themselves. The mechanics free condition added the requirement of translating their ordered ideas into a rough draft. The polished sentence condition further required correct spelling, punctuation, and so on. Thus, the polished sentence condition demanded attention to monitoring even at the level of mechanics as well as careful formulation and execution. Monitoring in the mechanics free condition was restricted to higher-level text concerns. The ordered proposition condition monitored only idea organization and permitted little if any attention to be paid to sentence generation. Finally, the unordered proposition condition lessened even the planning demands by focussing attention on idea generation while ignoring organization.

The results showed a systematic decline in the number of arguments generated across the four conditions as constraints increased. The unordered proposition instructions, which focused attention solely on generating, yielded more than three times as many arguments as the polished sentence instructions, which spread attention across all aspects of formulating, executing, and monitoring. Quality judgments of a second, final draft were not collected. However, the number of sentences, the number of clauses per sentence, and measures of mechanics were the same across conditions. The number of arguments presented per sentence, however, was lowest in the polished sentence condition. Writers who delayed their concern for organization, effective sentence construction, and careful editing on the first draft took care of these issues on the final draft.

Brown, McDonald, Brown and Carr (1988) manipulated the availability of sentences in the formulation system by visually presenting them to be copied in one case and requiring their recall in another. They also manipulated the execution and perhaps monitoring systems by stressing speed of handwriting in one case and legibility in another. They found that the legibility or execution accuracy was affected by both the availability and stress manipulations. When formulation must rely on memory retrieval, legibility decreased and both corrected and uncorrected errors increased. This implied interference in the execution system as a result of a direct manipulation of the difficulty of formulating sentences. It seemed unlikely that the decrement came from the monitoring system because both corrected and uncorrected errors showed the same advantage for copying as opposed to recalling the sentences. Brown et al. interpreted the above result to mean that formulation drew attention away from execution under the difficult recall conditions.

The trade-offs described here across diverse processes in writing offer preliminary support for the proposition that the central executive must be shared by formulation, execution, and monitoring processes. The claim is not that code specific components are irrelevant to writing, as will be seen next. Instead, multiple, code-specific components alone are not sufficient to account for the results obtained in text production. It is not apparent how verbal, visual, and spatial resources by themselves would explain the trade-offs observed between motor execution and planning.

Complex span
Another potential source of evidence comes from complex span measures of working memory and their relation to text comprehension and production. These require processing two tasks concurrently as well as the storage of information in short-term memory. It is arguable that tests of reading, speaking, writing, and math spans assess the capacity of the central executive in addition to or instead of verbal working memory. The math test in particular, although verbally encoded, requires the manipulation of mathematical symbols. So if math span correlates with text production ability, then one may argue that individual differences reflect the contribution of a general resource of working memory.

It is too early to tell what the span correlations say about the present model. For example, the greater one's working memory capacity as measured by reading span, the better one can select lexical items for use in a sentence in both adults and children (Daneman & Greene, 1986; McCutchen, Covill, Hoyne, and Mildes, 1994). Ransdell and her colleagues developed a writing span test in which sentences are produced, rather than comprehended, while storing words. She has found consistent positive relations between writing span and fluency, but when correlated with text quality the outcome is variable (Ransdell & Levy, 1996; Ransdell et al., 1998, also see Ransdell & Levy, this volume). Also, a set of tests that demanded reordering letters, words, and sentences (Benton, Kraft, Glover, & Plake, 1984) discriminated good from poor writers, whereas simple memory span tests did not.

But do these correlations inform us about the role of the verbal component, the central executive, or both in writing? The reading span test, for example, could be best characterized as an assessment of verbal working memory. In fact, Daneman and Merkile (1996) concluded that the most valid predictors of reading comprehension are span measures that include both a verbal storage and a verbal processing component. The math span test significantly predicts comprehension, implying that complex span indexes skill in manipulating and storing symbolic representations in general, not just linguistic symbols. This general skill may depend as much on the central executive as on verbal working memory. A study of math span in writing has apparently not yet been reported, so it is premature to say that the same pattern will be obtained in text production. The reordering tasks used by Benton et al. might easily be seen as requiring the central executive, but again the symbols manipulated were all verbal in nature.

Ideally, one would assess individual differences in each of the three postulated components and correlate these differences with writing performance. Without these assessments, or even with them, experiments that manipulate the availability of each component are needed to develop understanding of working memory in literacy.

3.2 Code-Specific Components

The second hypothesis is that code-specific components of working memory are differentially activated by formulation, execution, and monitoring processes. If that is so, then a concurrent task that loads a code-specific component of working memory, but not the central executive, should affect writing performance differently than one that loads both components. Ransdell, Levy, and Kellogg (1998; Experiment 1) loaded the verbal component of working memory but not the central executive by playing irrelevant speech while writers composed for 10 minutes. In Experiment 2, the writers listened for a tone in the otherwise irrelevant speech cueing them to shift attention to a target word that had to be categorized in terms of either its semantic, spatial, or phonological features. The response demands of this condition presumably added a slight load on the central executive relative to the irrelevant speech condition. In Experiment 3, the writers concurrently retained six digits, a task that substantially loaded the central executive along with verbal working memory.

Significant differences in fluency, measured in words per minute (WPM), were observed. Fluency dropped by about 2.5 WPM when ignoring irrelevant speech and by about 3.5 WPM when listening for tones embedded in the speech and categorizing target words. Similar effects were observed in the mean length of sentences generated. As can be seen in Table 2, the decline in fluency and sentence length was still more substantial for the six digit load of Experiment 3. This condition also significantly lowered the quality of the texts produced.

Lea and Levy (this volume) required either a visuospatial tracking task (the movements of an arrow in a box on the left side of a word processing screen) or a phonological task (monitoring for repetitions of a letter or digit name in the same left hand box). While doing these secondary tasks, the participants composed a text for 20 minutes as the primary task with a word processor. The results showed a

Table 2   *Effects of Concurrent Loads on Fluency and Sentence Length. Fluency is measured in the mean number words per minute and sentence length in the mean number of words per sentence. Standard deviations are given in parentheses.*

Condition	Fluency	Sentence Length
No Speech Control (Exp. 1; $\underline{N}$ = 34)	17.0 (5.7)	14.5 (5.0)
Irrelevant Speech (Exp. 1)	14.6 (4.9)	14.1 (5.4)
No Speech Control (Exp. 2; $\underline{N}$ = 67)	17.2 (7.8)	14.5 (5.8)
Irrelevant Speech Plus Decisions (Exp 2)	13.6 (7.1)	13.1 (5.6)
No Digits Control (Exp 3; $\underline{N}$ = 62)	17.1 (6.9)	14.6 (4.5)
Six Digits Retention (Exp. 3)	10.4 (4.7)	11.6 (5.0)

decline in text quality (about 15%) when either secondary task was performed. The accuracy on the secondary task declined reliably more relative to baseline on the phonological task than on the visuospatial task. The phonological task was harder to combine with writing because it demanded the verbal component of working memory, which was needed by both reading and translating. The visual/spatial component supported only planning and so was relatively less crucial. Another finding supporting this interpretation was the reduction in fluency observed in the two conditions. Words produced per minute declined by 13% in the visuospatial condition, but by 21% in the phonological condition. These data are the first to document that one can obtain different effects by loading the verbal versus the visual/spatial components of working memory during composition.

Thus, there is evidence that reducing the availability of specific components of working memory has unique effects on composing texts. One way to examine this hypothesis further is to simplify the composition task greatly by using a sentence generation task (Kellogg & Catterton, 1996). On each trial, the writer composed a single sentence that included two noun prompts. The purpose was to limit the scope of planning to idea generation alone and to minimize the degree and kind of monitoring needed. Previous research on spoken and written sentence production (Power, 1985; Jeffery & Underwood, 1995) suggested that a preload on verbal working memory (retaining three digits) should disrupt the degree of semantic work done during sentence formulation. This disruption should be less than that observed with a preload on both the central executive and the verbal component (six digits).

We extended these earlier studies by including a visualization condition taken from Podgorny and Shepard (1978) to preload the visual/spatial component, and by equating the response requirements across the conditions. The response requirements in the three and six digit conditions were greater than in the control condition in the earlier experiments. In the three digit and six digit conditions, the writers viewed a memory set, received a pair of nouns, and then wrote a sentence incorporating the nouns. This was followed by a recognition test for the digits requiring a binary response (yes, the test digits matched the memory set, or no they did not). In the visual image condition, the participants studied a block letter (e.g., L) presented on a 5 X 5 grid as a memory preload. At test, they viewed the same grid with one of the cells marked with a dark circle. They decided whether the circle coincided with one of the cells covered by the block letter L (e.g., the answer would be "yes" for the lower left cell, but "no" for the upper right cell). The control condition also required a yes response on every trial indicating that the asterisks presented in place of the digits matched at study and at test. The time taken to initiate and then type the sentence was recorded.

The load on working memory was varied within-subjects. Half of the participants received instructions to generate a simple sentence on each trial and the other half instructions to generate a complex sentence with an independent and a dependent clause. The expectation was that sentence production would degrade in varying degrees across conditions relative to a no load control condition. The six digit condition should cause the most problems, because it loads both the central executive and verbal working memory (see Table 1). The three digit condition should have loaded only the verbal component, and the image condition only the visual/spatial component. These should have caused significantly less disruption of sentence production than the six digit load, with the image condition in theory affecting only planning and the three digit condition only translating and reading.

It took significantly longer to generate a complex sentence (M = 3.75s) than a simple sentence (M = 2.53s), reflecting additional syntactic operations to translate the complex sentences. Unrelated nouns (M = 3.54s) required significantly more initiation time than related nouns (M = 2.74s), reflecting extra planning time. The relatedness effect and the complexity effect did not interact, suggesting that they affected independent stages of processing the sentences. The complexity difference presumably arose from the grammatical component of the translation process. The origin of the relatedness effect was probably in the planning of the message content (Bock & Levelt, 1994; Bock, 1995). The magnitude of the complexity effect and the relatedness effect were constant across the three preload conditions and the no load control. Initiation time also held steady across the various conditions.

The preload conditions significantly decreased the time taken to type sentences after initiation and the number of words generated per sentence. Shown in Table 3 are the means collapsed across the simple versus complex sentence variable. Sentences were presumably shorter because the loads on working memory reduced the amount of lexical-semantic work done in planning and translating the sentences. The six digit condition resulted in shortest typing time and sentences relative to the control condition; next came the three digit condition, followed by the image condition. This order is consistent with the model of Table 1 in that the six digit condition presumably disrupted planning, translating, reading, and editing. The three digit condition disrupted translating and reading, whereas the image condition disrupted only planning.

The syntactic output did not vary across the working memory conditions. For example, there were no more sentence fragments in the six digit load than in the control condition. Although not every sentence generated in the complex condition included a dependent clause, the average number of clauses generated did not vary across working memory loads. The sentence length effect thus supports the view that one can selectively disrupt writing processes. In particular this disruption most affected the lexical-semantic aspects of sentence generation rather than its syntactic aspects.

Levy and Marek (this volume) simplified the writing task still further by examining the formulation, execution, and monitoring processes separately. In their experiment on the formulation process, the writers viewed five words that could be

Table 3   *Effects of Working Memory Preloads on Typing Time and Sentence Length. The time values represent the mean of each individual's median time (s) in each condition. Sentence length is the mean number of words per sentence in each condition. Standard deviations are given in parentheses. N = 48.*

Preload Condition	Typing Time	Sentence Length
Control	13.9 (5.3)	8.8 (2.2)
Visual Image	13.5 (5.4)	8.6 (2.5)
Three Digits	13.2 (5.3)	8.4 (2.2)
Six Digits	12.7 (5.0)	8.2 (2.2)

rearranged and combined with function words generated as needed to form a sentence. This is a simplified sentence generation task not only because all the content words were provided but also because the experimenters tried to discourage the writers from generating their own grammatical inflections. Nouns were to be kept either singular or plural and the tenses of verbs were not to be changed from their presented form. In their execution experiment, the writers typed paragraphs of text presented to them as rapidly and as accurately as possible. In their monitoring experiment, the participants viewed a text of three paragraphs and highlighted errors. These included spelling errors, improper verb use, pronoun use, adverb use, sentence structure, and punctuation. In each experiment, they compared a silent control condition with an irrelevant speech condition.

On the assumption that irrelevant speech interferes with verbal working memory, but not with the central executive or other components, the model outlined in Table 1 provides a straightforward prediction. The irrelevant speech effect should have no impact in the execution and monitoring experiments, but it should interfere with even the simplified sentence generation task. The results neatly fit this prediction. The typing speed and errors and the proofreading errors were no different in the control and irrelevant speech conditions, despite ample statistical power to detect any significant variations. In contrast, the irrelevant speech decreased the percentage of target words used in the generated sentence, the percentage used in exactly the form provided by the experimenters, and the subjectively rated quality of the sentences produced compared to the silent control. Their results provide particularly convincing evidence that the process of constructing a sentence from given information is degraded when verbal working memory alone is concurrently loaded.

3.3 Long-Term Working Memory

The third hypothesis regarding working memory is that writers with expertise in a particular domain may expand their transient working memory capacity through reliable retrieval of knowledge from long-term memory. Ericsson and Kintsch (1995) made the intriguing claim that the limited capacity of transient working memory (ST-WM) can be circumvented by domain-specific knowledge in LT-WM. To the extent that writing expertise is governed by principles that characterize the performance of experts in other cognitive arenas, such as mental calculation, chess, or mnemonic skill (Torrance, 1996), then LT-WM may be necessary in a full account of how knowledge is used in text production. Ericsson and Kintsch further suggested that much of the evidence on capacity limitations could be reinterpreted in light of their proposal. Here the point to be made is that LT-WM may hypothetically play a crucial role in text production for highly knowledgeable writers. However, even these writers still must contend with the limitations discussed earlier that arise from the central executive and the code-specific components of working memory.

All existing theories of working memory in literacy skills have taken for granted that we are dealing with short-term, rather than long-term phenomena. A broader conception of working memory might consider selective access to well-learned facts and procedures in long-term memory as well. Ericsson and Delaney (in press) suggest that working memory be viewed as all mechanisms that support reliable access to information needed to complete a task. When so defined, it seems reasonable to include the retrieval structures used by experts to gain easy access to domain-specific knowledge as part of working memory. Conceivably, writers who know a topic well draw on long-term memory just as readily as less expert writers draw on transient working memory.

Expertise regarding the writing topic results in a more cohesive text (McCutchen, 1986) and a richer web of propositions generated and expressed in narrative texts (Voss, Vesonder, & Spillich, 1980). For example, Voss et al. compared individuals with a high versus a low degree of domain knowledge about baseball and then asked them to generate a narrative about a half inning of the game. In particular, the high knowledge writers included more relevant auxiliary as opposed to main game actions than did low knowledge writers.

Of interest here was whether the Voss et al. procedure would show that high knowledge writers produce texts judged to be of superior quality. If so, could such an effect be linked to their use of LT-WM. In two experiments the quality of texts written by high and low knowledge writers was judged using ratings of content and style (Kellogg, 1998). Content was defined in terms of how well ideas were developed, how coherently organized the text was, and how effectively the text communicated its message. Style was defined in terms of the quality of word choice, sentence structure, spelling, and grammar. The judges were trained to rate these traits on 7-point scales ranging from 1 (poor) to 7 (excellent). They rated typed versions of the texts. All of the students wrote both a baseball narrative, taken from Voss et al., and a persuasive editorial arguing for a million dollar per year cap on the salaries of professional baseball players; their task was to persuade the public that the current excessive salaries will ruin the national pastime. Half of the participants wrote the narrative first and the other half the persuasive.

In Experiment 1, writers with a high and low degree of verbal ability based on standardized achievement test scores were further divided into groups of high and low knowledge about baseball using the Voss et al. test (N = 61). The content and style ratings were strongly correlated and were affected the same by verbal ability and domain knowledge. They were, therefore, combined to yield an overall quality rating. The means are given in Table 4. The data are collapsed across the type of text, because the same effects were found for both narrative and persuasive assignments. The degree of verbal ability and domain-specific knowledge reliably improved the quality of the texts written and these factors did not interact. High verbal writers (M = 9.4) received higher quality scores than low verbal writers (M = 8.0). Similarly, high domain knowledge writers (M = 9.6) performed better than those with low knowledge (M = 7.8). These results reinforce earlier studies on the importance of knowledge availability in long-term memory for writers. The key question now is whether the writers with a strong knowledge of baseball had a reliable way to retrieve what they knew from long-term memory that differed from low knowledge writers. Did the high knowledge writers make use of a system of LT-WM?

If the quality effect of expertise is mediated by LT-WM, then the high knowledge writers ought to have greater spare capacity in working memory than low knowledge writers. If these writers gain access to their knowledge through LT-WM, with only the retrieval cues needing the resources of ST-WM, then they should be able to cope with extra demands on ST-WM relatively easily. Secondary task RT provides one way to assess this possibility. Increases in RT to detect a tone when one is writing relative to baseline provide a measure of cognitive effort or the relative momentary expenditure of attentional capacity (Kahneman, 1973). In the context of working memory, focusing attention on detecting the tone and scheduling a response makes demands on the central executive. If the executive functions of writers with a high degree of domain knowledge are relatively free to respond to the secondary signal, then less RT interference should be observed during composition.

In Experiment 2, interference with secondary RT was examined ($N = 48$). The design of Experiment 1 was replicated with the exception of adding the RT procedures used in earlier research (Kellogg, 1994). The overall quality ratings replicated the main effects and the lack of interaction between verbal ability and domain knowledge. As before, the quality measure was affected by verbal ability and domain knowledge in the same manner for both narrative and persuasive tasks. The knowledge effects are reliable and not restricted to a single type of discourse. Direct measurements of spare capacity in transient working memory showed that a high degree of domain-specific knowledge allowed for less interference on the RT task. (Table 4). That is, high domain knowledge writers ($M = 227$ ms) showed reliably less RT interference than did low knowledge writers ($M = 339$ ms). The same difference was observed in narrative and persuasive tasks. Similarly, verbal ability had no significant impact on the RT interference measure and it did not interact with domain knowledge. Thus, a high degree of domain-specific knowledge reduced the interference in secondary task RT observed during writing regardless of the verbal abilities of the individuals.

The results, then, offer preliminary evidence that Ericsson and Kintsch's view that domain-specific knowledge provides a system of working memory not considered in earlier models, specifically a system of LT-WM. It is worth noting that two experiments predating Ericsson and Kintsch's theory also manipulated domain specific knowledge in different ways from the current experiments and found significant declines in RT interference associated with a high degree of knowledge (Kellogg, 1987). One of these varied domain knowledge by selecting topics that were familiar and unfamiliar to college students. This design eliminates the possibility that writers possessing a high degree of domain knowledge happen to be

Table 4   Text Quality and RT Interference as a Function of Domain Knowledge and Verbal Ability.

Knowledge Condition	Text Quality	RT Interference (ms)
Experiment 1 (N=61)		
Low Domain Knowledge		
Low Verbal	7.1 (1.8)	-
High Verbal	8.4 (1.8)	-
High Domain Knowledge		
Low Verbal	8.8 (2.0)	-
High Verbal	10.3 (1.7)	-
Experiment 2 (N=42)		
Low Domain Knowledge		
Low Verbal	6.1 (2.6)	349 (166)
High Verbal	8.9 (1.6)	328 (164)
High Domain Knowledge		
Low Verbal	8.2 (1.6)	218 (146)
High Verbal	10.3 (1.9)	236 (121)

more intelligent, which in turn mediates the reduction in RT interference. Domain knowledge per se, not general aptitude, is responsible. Olive, Piolat, and Roussey (1996) reported an independent replication of this effect using the same familiar and unfamiliar topics for French rather than English writers.

4   CONCLUSION

Three hypotheses on the relation of working memory to writing were explored here. The first asserts that a central executive component is indispensable in understanding text production. Virtually all of the basic processes of the formulation, execution, and monitoring systems are resource limited with respect to executive functions. In support of this first proposition are data implying trade-offs among formulation, execution, and monitoring processes.

The second hypothesis is that multiple code-specific components of transient working memory are also essential to explaining text production. It assumes that the central executive functions are complemented by components that process and store specific kinds of mental representations. At a minimum, these include verbal (phonological) and visual/spatial components. The argument for this claim rests on evidence suggesting that loads on verbal working memory degrade writing performance differently than do loads on visual/spatial and central executive components.

The final hypothesis is that working memory is not restricted to transient components that temporarily process and store information. Ericsson and Kintsch's (1995) insights on LT-WM may help in understanding the ability of writers highly knowledgeable in a domain to retrieve and apply what they know to problems of a writing task. Domain-specific knowledge that is reliably accessible from long-term memory expands what is otherwise a transient, limited capacity system of working memory. Preliminary support for this view comes from experiments showing that a high degree of knowledge about a writing topic reduces the degree of interference observed in secondary probe RT during composition. The executive functions of a high domain knowledge writer seem to be less overloaded by the writing task and more readily able to detect and respond to the secondary probe.

The first two hypotheses stem from the model of transient working memory and writing outlined in Table 1 and described in Kellogg (1996). This model assumes a three component system of working memory after Baddeley (1986). The evidence reviewed here adds further support to the model's predictions, but detailed tests of its assumptions are clearly needed in future research. Although the central executive, verbal, and visual/spatial components appear useful in explaining text production, it probably will be necessary to add components.

Already there is evidence from other areas of working memory research showing that spatial and visual components are separate systems, and that a semantic component looks plausible (Jonides & Smith, 1997; Logie, 1986). The semantic component processes and stores abstract, propositional representations and would seem especially important in planning ideas and reflecting on the content and rhetorical problems of a given writing task (Hayes, 1996). Graphemic codes may also be stored and processed in a specialized component of working memory (Caramazza & Miceli, 1990). Lastly, a component of working memory linked to long-term rather than short-term storage may be worth examining (Ericsson & Kintsch, 1995). This novel form of working memory may be critical to our understanding of how experts bring their domain-specific knowledge to bear on the content problems of writing.

AUTHOR NOTE

I wish to thank Michael Levy for his helpful suggestions on an earlier draft of this chapter.

REFERENCES

Baddeley, A. D. (1986). *Working memory*. Oxford: Oxford University Press.

Benton, S. L., Corkill, A. J., Sharp, J. M., Downey, R. G., & Khramtsova, I. (1995). Knowledge, interest, and narrative writing. *Journal of Educational Psychology, 87*, 66-79.

Benton, S. L., Kraft, R. G., Glover, J. A., & Plake, B. S. (1984). Cognitive capacity differences among writers. *Journal of Educational Psychology, 76*, 820-834.

Bock, J. K. (1982). Toward a cognitive psychology of syntax: Information processing contributions to sentence formulation. *Psychological Review, 89*, 1-47.

Bock, J. K. (1995), Sentence production: From mind to mouth. In J. L. Miller & P. D. Eimas (Eds.), *Handbook of perception and cognition: Speech, language, and communication* Vol. 11, pp. 181-216). San Diego: Academic Press.

Bock, J. K., & Levelt, W. J. M. (1994). Language production: Grammatical encoding. In M. A. Gernsbacher (Ed.), *Handbook of psycholinguistics* (pp. 945-984). San Diego: Academic Press.

Bourdin, B., & Fayol, M. (1994). Is written language production more difficult than oral language production. A working memory approach. *International Journal of Psychology, 29*, 591-620.

Bourdin, B., & Fayol, M. (1996). Mode effects in a sentence production task. *Current Psychology of Cognition, 15*, 245-264.

Broadbent, D. E. (1958). *Perception and communication*. London: Pergamon Press.

Brown, J. S., McDonald, J. L., Brown, T. L., & Carr, T. H. (1988). Adapting to processing demands in discourse production: The case of handwriting. *Journal of Experimental Psychology: Human Perception and Performance, 14*, 45-59.

Caramazza, A., & Miceli, G. (1990). The structure of graphemic representations. *Cognition, 37*, 243-297.

Cowan, N. (1995). *Attention and memory: An integrated framework*. New York: Oxford University Press.

Daneman, M., & Greene, I. (1986). Individual differences in comprehending and producing words in context. *Journal of Memory and Language, 25*, 1-18.

Daneman, M., & Merikle, P. M. (1996). Working memory and language comprehension: A meta-analysis. *Psychonomic Bulletin & Review, 3*, 422-434.

Engle, R. W., Cantor, J., & Carullo, J. J. (1992). Individual differences in working memory and comprehension: Test of four hypotheses. *Journal of Experimental Psychology: Learning, Memory, & Cognition, 18*, 972-992.

Ericsson, K. A., & Delaney, P. F. (in press). Long-term working memory as an alternative to capacity models of working memory in everyday skilled performance. In A. Miyake and P. Shah (Eds.) *Models of working memory*. Cambridge, UK: Cambridge University Press.

Ericsson, K. A., & Kintsch, W. (1995). Long-term working memory. *Psychological Review, 102*, 211-245.

Fayol, M. (1991). From sentence production to text production: Investigating fundamental processes. *European Journal of Psychology of Education, 6 (2)*, 101-119.

Fayol, M., Largy, P., & Lemaire, P. (1994). When cognitive overload enhances subject-verb agreement errors. *The Quarterly Journal of Experimental Psychology, 47A*, 437-464.

Fitzgerald, J. (1987). Research on revision in writing. *Review of Educational Research, 57*, 481-506.

Flower, L., & Hayes, J. R. (1980). The dynamics of composing: Making plans and juggling constraints. In L. W. Gregg & E. R. Steinberg (Eds.), *Cognitive processes in writing* (pp. 31-50). Hillsdale, NJ: Lawrence Erlbaum Associates.

Garrett, M. F. (1980). Levels of processing in sentence production. In B. Butterworth (Eds.), *Language production* (pp. 177-220). London: Academic Press.

Gathercole, S. E., & Baddeley, A. D. (1993). *Working memory and language.* Hillsdale, NJ: Lawrence Erlbaum Associates.

Glynn, S. M., Britton, B. K., Muth, D., & Dogan, N. (1982). Writing and revising persuasive documents: Cognitive demands. *Journal of Educational Psychology, 74,* 557-567.

Graham, S. & Harris, K. R. (1997). Self-regulation and writing: Where do we go from here. *Contemporary Educational Psychology, 22,* 102-114.

Graham, S. (1990). The role of production factors in learning disabled students' compositions. *Journal of Educational Psychology, 82,* 781-791.

Graham, S., Beringer, V. W., Abbot, R. D., Abbot, S. P., & Whitaker, D. (1997). Role of mechanics in composing of elementary school students: A new methodological approach. *Journal of Educational Psychology, 89,* 170-182.

Hayes, J. R. (1996). A new framework for understanding cognition and affect in writing. In C. Michael Levy and S. Ransdell (Eds.), *The science of writing: Theories, methods, individual differences and applications* (pp. 1-27). Mahwah, NJ: Erlbaum Associates.

Hayes, J. R., & Flower, L. S. (1980). Identifying the organization of writing processes. In L. W. Gregg & E. R. Steinberg (Eds.), *Cognitive processes in writing* (pp. 3-30). Hillsdale, NJ: Lawrence Erlbaum Associates.

Jeffery, G. C., & Underwood, G. (1995, January). *The role of working memory in sentence production.* Paper presented at the annual meeting of the Experimental Psychology Society, London.

Jeffery, G., & Underwood, G. (1996). Writing as problem solving: The role of concrete and abstract knowledge in the production of written text. In G. Rijlaarsdam, J. van den Bergh, and M. Couzijn (Eds.), *Theories, models and methodology in writing research* (pp. 61-86). Amsterdam: Amsterdam University Press.

Jonides, J., & Smith, E. E. (1997). The architecture of working memory. In M. D. Rugg (Ed.) *Cognitive Neuroscience* (pp. 243-276). Cambridge, MA: MIT Press.

Just, M. A. & Carpenter, P. A. (1992) A capacity theory of comprehension: Individual differences in working memory. *Psychological Review, 99,* 122-149.

Kahneman, D. (1973), *Attention and effort.* Englewood Cliffs, NJ: Prentice-Hall.

Kellogg, R. T. (1987). Effects of topic knowledge on the allocation of processing time and cognitive effort to writing processes. *Memory & Cognition, 15,* 256-266.

Kellogg, R. T. (1988). Attentional overload and writing performance: Effects of rough draft and outline strategies. *Journal of Experimental Psychology: Learning, Memory, and Cognition, 14,* 355-365.

Kellogg, R. T. (1994). *The psychology of writing.* New York: Oxford University Press.

Kellogg, R. T. (1996). A model working memory in writing. In C. Michael Levy and S. Ransdell (Eds.), The science of writing: Theories, methods, individual differences and applications (pp. 57-71). Mahwah, NJ: Erlbaum Associates.

Kellogg, R. T. (1998, May). *Long-term working memory in text production.* Paper presented at the annual meeting of the American Psychological Society, Washington, DC.

Kellogg, R. T., & Catterton, K. (1996, November). *Working memory in the production of written sentences.* Paper presented at the annual meeting of the Psychonomic Society, Chicago.

Levelt, W. J. M. (1989). *Speaking: From intention to articulation.* Cambridge, MA: MIT Press.

Logie, R. H. (1986). Visuo-spatial processing in working memory. *Quarterly Journal of Experimental Psychology, 38A,* 229-247.

Martin, R. C., Shelton, J. R., & Yaffee, L. S. (1994). Language processing and working memory: Neuropsychological evidence for separate phonological and semantic capabilities. *Journal of Memory and Language, 33,* 83-111.

McCutchen, D. (1986). Domain knowledge and linguistic knowledge in the development of writing ability. *Journal of Memory and Language, 25,* 431-444.

McCutchen, D. (1996). A capacity theory of writing: Working memory in composition. *Educational Psychology Review, 8,* 299-325.

McCutchen, D., Covil, A., Hoyne, S. H., & Mildes, K. (1994). Individual differences in writing: Implications of translating fluency. *Journal of Educational Psychology, 86,* 256-266.

Norman, D. A., & Bobrow, D. G. (1975). On data-limited and resource-limited processes. *Cognitive Psychology, 7*, 44-64.

Nystrand, M. (1982). (Ed.). *What writers know: The language, process, and structure of written discourse.* New York: Academic Press.

Olive, T., Piolat, A., & Roussey, J. Y. (1996, September). *The effect of the degree of expertise and the level of knowledge on cognitive effort associated to writing processes.* Paper presented at the meeting of the Writing Special Interest Group of the European Association of Research on Learning and Instruction, Barcelona.

Paivio, A. (1986). *Mental representations: A dual coding approach.* New York: Oxford University Press.

Piolat, A. (1998). Planning and text quality among undergraduate Students: Findings and Questions. In M. Torrance and D. Galbraith (Eds.) *Knowing what to write: Conceptual processes in text production.* Amsterdam: Amsterdam University Press.

Piolat, A., Roussey, J. Y., Olive, T., & Farioli, F. (1996). Charge mentale et mobilisation des processus rédactionnels: examen de la procédure de Kellogg. *Psychologie Française, 41*, 339-354.

Podgorny, P. & Shepard, R. N. (1978). Functional representations common to visual perception and imagination. *Journal of Experimental Psychology: Human Perception and Performance, 4*, 21-35.

Power, M. J. (1985). Sentence production and working memory. *The Quarterly Journal of Experimental Psychology, 37A*, 367-385.

Ransdell, S., & Levy, C. M. (1996). Working memory constraints on writing quality and fluency. In C. M. Levy & S. Ransdell (Eds.). *The science of writing: Theories, methods, individual differences, and applications.* Mahwah, NJ: Erlbaum Associates.

Ransdell, S., Levy, C. M., & Kellogg, R. T. (1998). *Concurrent loads on working memory during text production.* Manuscript submitted for publication.

Rau, P. S., & Sebrechts, M. M. (1996). How initial plans mediate the expansion and resolution of options in writing. *Quarterly Journal of Experimental Psychology, 49A*, 616-638.

Sadowski, M., Kealy, W. A., Goetz, E. T., & Paivio, A. Concreteness and imagery effects in the written composition of definitions. *Journal of Educational Psychology, 89*, 518-526.

Scardamalia, M., & Bereiter, C. (1986). Written composition. In M. Wittrock (Ed.), *Handbook of research on teaching.* (3rd ed., pp. 778-803). New York: MacMillan.

Schoonen, R., & de Glopper, K. (1996). Writing performance and knowledge about writing. In G. Rijlaarsdam, H. van den Bergh, and M. Couzijn (Eds.), *Theories, models and methodology in writing research* (pp. 87-107) Amsterdam: Amsterdam University Press.

Shah, P. & Miyake, A. (1996). The separability of working memory resources for spatial thinking and language processing: An individual differences approach. *Journal of Experimental Psychology: General, 125*, 4-27.

Shallice, T., & Burgess, P. (1991). Deficits in strategy application following frontal lobe damage in man. *Brain, 114*, 727-741.

Shepard, R. N. (1978). The mental image. *American Psychologist, 33*, 125-137.

Stein, N. L. (1986). Knowledge and process in the acquisition of writing skills. *Review of Research in Education, 13*, 225-258.

Torrance, M. (1996). Is writing expertise like other kinds of expertise. In G. Rijlaarsdam, H. van den Bergh, and M. Couzijn (Eds.), *Theories, models and methodology in writing research* (pp. 3-9). Amsterdam: Amsterdam University Press.

Voss, J. F., Vesonder, G. T., & Spillich, G. J. (1980). Text generation and recall by high-knowledge and low-knowledge individuals. *Journal of Verbal Learning and Verbal Behavior, 17*, 651-667.

Wright, R. E. & Rosenberg, S. (1993). Knowledge of text coherence and expository writing: A developmental study. *Journal of Educational Psychology, 85*, 152-158.

Zimmerman, B., & Risemberg, R. (1997). Becoming a proficient writer: A self-regulatory perspective. *Contemporary Educational Psychology, 22*, 73-101.

Working Memory as a Resource in the Writing Process

Joseph Lea & C. Michael Levy
University of Florida, USA

ABSTRACT

Until recently, writing researchers seldom have made serious contact with mainstream research in cognitive psychology. We review four major classes of cognitive processing models that might serve as theoretical bases for extension to written language production. Then we focus on a set of three experiments that attempt to assess the merits of a reconceptualization of Kellogg's important new model by emphasizing the role of resource pools rather than binary functioning cognitive structures. Empirical findings support the recent trend toward multicomponent classes of working memory or resource models, particularly those that distinguish between visuospatial and verbal/phonological processing. Our results also indicate that there is a significant visuospatial component involved in text production.

1   INTRODUCTION

Research on cognitive capacity and writing is relatively new compared with studies of capacity limitations in reading, and to spoken language production and comprehension (see Gathercole and Baddeley, 1992 for an overview), obligating writing researchers to develop and refine appropriate models necessary for theoretical development and testing. Fortunately, the nature of human processing and storage limitations has long interested psychologists working within an information processing framework, and accounts of other language production tasks have developed constructs such as working memory, resource capacity, and mental workload.

Four theoretical candidates for a model of written language production are introduced below, followed by a critical analysis of information processing theory development, and rationale for the formation of a hybrid model. Readers familiar with the attention literature may wish to proceed to the section entitled, "Working Memory in Writing."

Structural theories were popularized in the 1950s with experimental investigations of the dichotic listening task, which revealed that attention was severely limited (Cherry, 1953; Broadbent, 1958; Moray, 1959). Several classes of theoretical models were generated to localize the point in information processing where the bottleneck occurs. Early-selection theories claimed that this bottleneck is in the early processes such as perception, and late-selection theories pointed to stages of decision making and response selection as the limiting stages of information processing.

The simplest framework for interpreting the demands placed on the writer postulates an *undifferentiated capacity* of mental resources (Kahneman, 1973). Performance on any given task declines only when the aggregate of task demands exceeds the capacity of resources.

An alternate conception of this resource economy distinguishes among the types of resources available at any given moment. This *multiple resource* model suggests that there may be various types of resources and that different tasks may require different types of resources in various compositions. The most prevalent distinction of resources is that between visuospatial and verbal resources, which extends the concept of "resources" to a neurologically plausible account of information processing (Wickens, 1984; Friedman & Polson, 1981). Friedman and Polson (1981) suggest that the physically distinct cerebral hemispheres can be seen as independent resource systems. The left and right hemispheres may form a system of two mutually inaccessible and finite pools of resources.

The Baddeley and Hitch (1974) model of working memory is a multi-component system for both the storage and the processing of verbal and visuospatial tasks. It has three primary components: a limited-capacity central executive and two peripheral slave systems. One of these slave systems, the phonological loop, handles verbal and auditory information. The other, the visuospatial sketchpad, is specialized for processing visual and spatial information.

As a writer plans ideas and translates them into prose, or types or manually writes sentences, while monitoring all of these activities, considerable demands are placed on temporary storage and processing capacity. A common assumption is that processing and storage capacity is divided between verbal and visuospatial components, which make separate contributions to the task at hand (Wickens, 1984; Baddeley & Hitch, 1974). We seek to provide an account of the division of labor between visuospatial and verbal processing demands and capacity limitations as they influence the writing process. In our approach, special treatment will be given to the dual-task methods.

We also extend the debates in the working memory and attention literature to the domain of writing research. Recently, working memory has become regarded as another way of talking about attentional resources. Baddeley's working memory model, however, differs from similar multiple resource models in that the phonological loop and the visuospatial sketchpad are assumed to process as structural rather than capacity components. The implications of this difference are discussed later. The balance of this section critically reviews the literature regarding the models just introduced, focusing on their assumptions about the nature of human cognitive limitations.

We believe that the literature regarding human cognitive limitations can illuminate the context in which models of writing exist. We will describe the implications our theoretical assumptions have both for the design and for the interpretation and generalizability of results from dual-task experiments. The review concludes with a summary and critique of existing literature and a proposal for an adapted theory of working memory that is tested in Experiment 1. We also present guidelines that we believe will be useful for future studies comparing the roles of the visuospatial sketchpad and phonological loop. Experiments 2 and 3 compare the involvement of phonological and visuospatial processing in essay writing.

2   RESOURCE CAPACITY VERSUS STRUCTURES

Two hypothetical constructs underlie each of the theoretical candidates just introduced. First, consider the capacity notion of *limited processing resources* that are demanded by non-automatic tasks. According to this view, performance declines only when the aggregate of task demands exceeds the limited capacity of resources. For example, when someone uses a word processor to translate an idea into text, it might be reasonable to expect that the requirement to simultaneously generate new ideas and edit grammatical and spelling mistakes would cause a disruption in the rate at which text is generated. Juggling that writing task with talking on the telephone or listening to the radio might further drive down performance. A second construct proposed to explain processing efficiency is referred to as *structure* (Pashler & Johnston, 1989). According to a structural view, when people attempt to simultaneously engage in competing mental operations, incompatible stages or processes are initiated, causing interference between tasks. That is, two tasks will compete when they each simultaneously require a single common process. For example, if two computers try to print a document at the same time using the same printer, only one printing task will be printed at a time. With people, an analogous situation might arise when someone attempts to talk on the telephone while simultaneously listening to a radio interview. This would be a more difficult dual-task combination than carrying on a conversation while riding a bike, presumably because producing and comprehending audible speech demands similar processes.

Two classes of theoretical models of attention have emerged from consideration of these hypothetical variables. These are *capacity* or *resource theories*, usually identified with Kahneman (1973), and *structural theories*, which began with Broadbent (1958) and recently have been elaborated by Pashler and his associates (Pashler & Johnston, 1989; Pashler & Carrier, 1995). After considering structural and capacity theories in more detail, we will argue that multiple resource models and Baddeley's working memory model each offer a rapprochement of structural and capacity theories. Further, Experiment 1 will reveal empirical findings suggesting that writing research may be best guided by a model that combines the strengths of both working memory and multiple resource theories.

2.1 Capacity Theories

How is it that we may become less conscious – rather than become entirely unaware – of some things when we become more conscious of others? Capacity theories seek to explain this common experience by suggesting that some resource pool is approaching its limitation. Thus, when a primary task demands more of these resources, fewer are available for a concurrent secondary task. The interest of human factors psychologists in the measurement of operator workload led to Knowles' (1963) conceptualization of the human operator as processing a pool of limited-capacity resources. Whereas structural theories assume that structures are dedicated to one task at a time, this alternate view assumes that capacity can be allocated between separate activities in graded quantity.

A conceptual model asserting that workload is proportional to the demands imposed by tasks on the operator's limited capacity was very attractive to many engineering psychologists. Those concerned with the measurement of the human operator workload applied the capacity model in settings such as aircraft cockpit design (Rolfe, 1971). Since the late 1970's, capacity theories have been applied to the presentation and measurement of resource capacity and to the relation between capacity-based workload measures, such as reaction time to a stimulus presented during performance of a primary task (probe RT paradigm) and alternative measures, such as subjective ratings and physiological parameters (Moray, 1982; Moray, Johannsen, Pew, Rasmusses, Sanders, & Wickens, 1979).

Nearly all of the original paradigms investigating the nature of resources (or mental capacity or effort) involve presenting two tasks to an individual to process simultaneously. These are known as dual-task experiments. Resource theories in large part were created to explain instances where two processes were simultaneously activated. Perhaps the earliest task (although not a traditional dual-task) was the Stroop task, where reading processes compete with color naming processes for a common pathway. Although theorizing about pathways has evolved into structural theories of attention, the basic question about mechanisms of interference is the same. In the 1950s British psychologists Broadbent, Moray, and others began using the dichotic listening task to test various structural models of the selection of attention; for example, late versus early selection. The probe technique emerged shortly thereafter (Posner & Bois, 1971), where participants respond to a discrete stimulus while performing some primary task. A participant's baseline reaction time was subtracted from his or her reaction time to a tone presented during performance of a primary task in order to compute an interference reaction time, which was assumed to be an index of mental effort.

Kahneman (1973) brought unity to the concept of capacity as an intervening variable in dual-task performance. His ideas and synthesis of the research at that time facilitated the evolution of the resource metaphor from an intuition to a quantitative theory with testable predictions. Since the early 1970s, capacity theories have continued to influence basic research in learning, memory, and writing as well as applied research where workload measurement is investigated. Capacity theories have, however, not gone without challenge from those who argue for a structural approach.

2.2 Structural Theories

Early studies of the limitations of attention often involved the dichotic presentation of verbal material. Subjects typically wore stereo headphones, through which different messages were simultaneously presented to each ear. Participants attended to one of the two messages and repeated it aloud immediately after hearing it (shadowing). This technique ensured that the participants focused on one of the two messages. Experimental investigations revealed that attention was severely limited (Cherry, 1953; Broadbent, 1958; Moray, 1959). Several classes of theoretical models were generated to localize the point in information processing where the apparent bottleneck occurred. Early-selection theories claimed that the bottleneck was in the early processes such as perception, and late-selection theories pointed to stages of decision making and response selection as the limiting stages of information processing.

Another paradigm was also often used in the investigation of the limitations of attention. The psychological refractory period (PRP) paradigm (Bertelson, 1967; Welford, 1967), also known as the overlapping tasks paradigm (Pashler, 1984), involves the presentation of two stimuli (S1 and S2) in rapid succession. Participants make a response to each stimulus (R1 and R2) as quickly as possible. Using this paradigm, many researchers (Kantowitz, 1974; Pashler, 1984; Pashler & Johnston, 1989; Fagot & Pashler, 1992) concluded, as did the late-selection theorists, that limitations in processing were localized in the response initiation phase.

Subsequent extension of this structural model by the late-selection theorists (Deutsch & Deutsch, 1963; Mackay, 1973; Johnston & Heinz, 1978) postulated that there is not a single stage or mental operation that acts as the source of interference. Instead, a limited-capacity central processor, when engaged by one task, is unavailable to a second task requiring the same operation. Thus the performance of the second task will necessarily deteriorate. By suggesting that there are a number of operations that require the exclusive attention of the limited-capacity central processor in order to proceed, this view permits more than one bottleneck in the information processing system. Restrictions in the ability to carry on multiple mental computations can occur at a variety of stages, including perceptual identification, decision and response selection, response initiation and execution (Pashler & Johnston, 1989), and motor mechanisms (Kahneman, 1973).

Broadbent (1982) criticized studies of continuous performance that rely on accuracy measures because they cannot discriminate between the predictions of capacity theory regarding simultaneous mental processing of both tasks and the predictions of structural models regarding strategy switching strategy. Pashler and Johnston (1989) incorporated Broadbent's suggestions when they investigated dual-task interference with the PRP. They argued that this paradigm potentially provides much more detailed information about the time course of dual-task interference than is obtained in continuous dual-task studies.

Pashler and Johnston divided models of dual task interference into two categories: (a) capacity sharing models discussed earlier and (b) postponement models. In postponement models, some bottleneck stage or process cannot operate simultaneously for each of two overlapping tasks. As a result, processing of this stage in the second task is literally postponed. This produces the relatively straightforward hypothesis that as stimulus onset asynchrony (SOA) between S1 and S2 is reduced, there should come a point at which any further reduction in the SOA produces a corresponding increase in the duration of R2. However, even when this prediction is confirmed, it does not seem to contradict predictions from the capacity theory.

A major finding that has frequently been observed with the overlapping tasks paradigm is a slowing of the R1 relative to single task performance (Kahneman, 1973). Similar findings in discrete movement research are thought to indicate the increased effort needed to compile a more complex movement (Henry & Rogers, 1960). R2 slowing is readily accounted for with the capacity models because both tasks are assumed to be performed with depleted allocations of capacity. Postponement models, in contrast, do not predict this slowing directly. It has been suggested that R1 slowing may result from a grouping strategy in which the subject essentially treats S1 and S2 as a compound stimulus and selects a corresponding compound response (Pashler & Johnston, 1989). Other strategies have been proposed as well, but in any case, R1 slowing alone is not thought to be especially diagnostic of the underlying causes of dual-task interference.

Kahneman (1973) claimed that a single-channel theory and the general limited capacity theory might account for the same findings. He observed that the assumptions of the single-channel theory are more restricting than the limited capacity models, and that predictions, especially for the PRP, have typically failed to be confirmed. Pashler and Johnston concede that the PRP paradigm has been studied less in recent years, leaving unresolved the debate between structural and capacity theories. Because both capacity and structural models offer a plausible account of the basic results, analytic tests that make distinctive, non-obvious predictions are necessary before this debate can be resolved.

2.3 Multiple Resource Theories

A search for a resolution to the structure/capacity debate led directly to multiple resource models (Navon & Gopher, 1979), where resources are declared to reside within structures or pools. Until multiple resource models emerged, interference was thought to depend exclusively on either the extent to which two tasks draw on a common resource pool or to structural limitations, where some stage of processing cannot proceed in parallel with another. Neither of these accounts explains all of the phenomena related to interference. The central capacity hypothesis cannot explain why some secondary tasks interfere more with one primary task than another equally difficult primary task. For example, vocal responses interfere more than spatial responses with the recall of sentences, but less than spatial responses with recall of line diagrams (Brooks, 1968). Pure structural models are also inadequate because processes that share similar stages or mechanisms may interfere with each other, but they seldom block each other completely (Navon & Gopher, 1979). For example, when Triesman and Davies (1973) presented participants simultaneously with stimuli to the same modality, performance was impaired, but not entirely impeded.

Multiple resource theory claims that there may be various types of resources and that different tasks may require different types of resources in various compositions (Navon & Gopher, 1979; Norman & Bobrow, 1975; Wickens, 1984). This approach is, on the one hand, structural because it identifies the source of interference as overlapping mechanisms. On the other hand, multiple resource theory is a capacity approach, because it does not assume that a mechanism can be accessed and used by only one process at a time. Rather, mechanisms have a capacity that can be shared by several processes until those processes demand more resources than the capacity allows. Thus, multiple resource theory is a union of capacity and structural models where structure is important, but each structure is limited by its own capacity. Despite its appeal, there are critics.

Navon and Gopher (1979) noted that multiple resource theory might leave researchers disconcerted by the prospect of devaluation of the time-honored concept of attention and that the proliferation of resources might seem strange or threatening. Those who favour the more conservative central capacity theory argue that multiple resource theory is not logically falsifiable and that it is impossible to know how many resource pools there are (Navon, 1984).Therefore, new resource pools could be postulated to account for any pattern of results. Multiple resource theory is class of models, however, and at that level it may not need to be falsifiable to be worthwhile. Rather than struggling to find a critical test for multiple resource theory, researchers might better focus on generating and testing specific models that delineate the composition of resources.

Wickens (1984) proposed a multiple resource model that accounts for a great deal of the dual-task data. Wickens assumes that the extent to which two tasks share common resource pools determines how much they will interfere in a dual-task paradigm. In particular, his resource architecture contains three dimensions derived from traditional psychological dichotomies: (a) Based on the general finding that it is easier to time-share an auditory and visual task than two auditory or two visual tasks, Wickens proposed a separation of resource pools specialized for dealing with different *processing modalities*. (b) The *processing codes* dimension distinguishes information that is spatial or analogue from that which is verbal or linguistic. (c) Wickens proposed a separation of *processing stages* based on the finding that tasks demanding either response processes or cognitive/perceptual processes will interfere with each other to a greater extent than will a perceptual and a response task.

2.4 Working Memory

Like the multiple resource approach, the Baddeley and Hitch (1974) model of working memory is another variation of structural and capacity models. Rather than resources within structures, this model implies both resource and structural components. The model's hybrid nature often goes overlooked, perhaps because working memory emerged from empirical research conducted on speech production, vocabulary acquisition, and speech comprehension rather than the typical lower level cognitive studies of processing limits where the capacity/structure debate flourished. Working memory has recently become a popular construct in writing research because speech production, vocabulary acquisition and speech comprehension presumably share some characteristics with written language production.

The Baddeley model evolved when neurological and experimental data did not fit assumptions concerning the functioning of the unitary short-term store in the modal model (Atkinson & Shiffrin, 1968). In the modal model, the short term store (STS) was positioned as the route information must take to gain access into a long-term store (LTS), but neurological evidence indicated that poor performance on an auditory memory span task was not linked to a long-term learning deficit (Shallice & Warrington, 1970). Nor did an impairment in the STS interfere with comprehension and production of speech (Vallar & Baddeley, 1984). Second, the short-term store was considered to play a major role in retrieval from the long-term store. However, a digit span task, performed concurrently with the retrieval phase of a free recall task, did not depress accuracy of retrieval (Baddeley, Lewis, & Vallar, 1984). Neither did rehearsal of a six digit number influence recall of paired associates (Baddeley, Thomson, & Buchanan, 1975). Third, a key postulate of the modal model was that the probability of information being transferred to long-term store was heightened by increased rehearsal. Yet, the time spent rehearsing target items interspersed at varying intervals in a longer list of words was unrelated to recall (Craik & Watkins, 1973). Nor did frequent rehearsal prior to the start of a free recall experiment improve recall of the rehearsed items (Tulving, 1966). Finally, another tenet of the modal model was that the recency effect in free recall tasks resulted from information remaining in the short-term store. This was inconsistent with findings that the recency effect remained even when participants counted backwards by three's for 20 seconds after each word (Tzeng & Hitch, 1977).

Baddeley's model is a multi-component system for both the storage and the processing of verbal and visuospatial tasks. It has three primary components: a limited-capacity central executive and two peripheral slave systems. One of these slave systems handles verbal and auditory information (the phonological loop). The other is specialized for visual and spatial information (the visuospatial sketchpad). These slave systems do not represent pools of limited resources that can act in parallel like the central executive. Instead, they operate serially, in the same sense that a computer's printer may receive multiple print jobs, but can only perform one print job at a time.

The phonological loop is assumed to be most important in the production, comprehension, and development of language. Architecturally, it has two subcomponents: (a) a phonological store that is believed to hold phonological information for approximately 2 seconds and (b) an articulatory mechanism that is implicated in the transfer of written verbal material to the phonological loop. Because the working memory model emerged from research on verbal tasks, the phonological loop has received much more study than either the central executive or the visuospatial sketchpad. There are five empirical sources of support for the phonological loop. First, evidence for the articulatory control process comes from the word length effect: memory span is smaller for long words than for short words. This is assumed to occur because rehearsal takes longer for longer words than for short words, allowing more decay to occur before the next rehearsal cycle. It is typically found that people remember as many words as they can read in 2 seconds (Baddeley, Thomson, & Buchanan, 1975). Second, performance is disrupted when participants vocalize some predefined pattern of speech (e.g., tee tah, tee tah) while they simultaneously perform some primary task. This articulatory suppression is claimed to engage the phonological store and block its ability to participate in accomplishing the primary task. Disruptions have been observed in a variety of tasks, including vocabulary acquisition and serial learning (Baddeley, Lewis, & Vallar, 1984). Third, performance degradation occurs when participants attempt to perform a primary task while irrelevant speech is presented that they are instructed to ignore. This procedure has been shown to disrupt serial recall of visually presented lists (Salame' & Baddeley, 1982a,b). Fourth, acoustic or phonological similarity effects are common where the dissimilar sounding items are recalled better than similar sounding items is interpreted as evidence that the phonological store is speech-based. Words or non-words that sound alike interfere with each other in memory span tests more than semantically related words that differ in their acoustic properties. Fifth, and most controversial at the moment, neuropsychological patients frequently have specific phonological loop deficits, but suffer no general cognitive impairment (Baddeley, Papagno, & Vallar, 1988).

The visuospatial sketchpad has been less researched than the phonological loop. Where phonological similarity effects have been observed in tasks believed to require the phonological loop, visual similarity effects have been observed in visuospatial tasks. It is common for stimuli that look alike to interfere with each other. Hue and Ericsson (1988) observed this phenomenon with Chinese characters in a study using participants who presumably had no experience with the Chinese language. Frick (1988) elaborated on the visual similarity effect, arguing on the basis of the frequency of errors like "P" being mistaken for "R" that images in visuospatial working memory are unparsed. Further evidence for the existence of the visuospatial sketchpad comes from neuropsychological studies where patients with right posterior lesions can be markedly impaired on tests of memory span for movements to different spatial locations, despite having normal auditory-verbal memory spans (De Renzi & Nichelli, 1975). Additionally, selective interference effects have been observed where concurrent visuospatial pursuit tracking disrupted performance on Brook's (1968) spatial task, but not on a corresponding abstract task (Baddeley, Thomson & Buchannon,1975).

The visuospatial sketchpad may also be involved in planning and executing spatial tasks. For example, Japanese abacus experts can perform complex calculations without the aid of the abacus, and appear to do so by simulating the apparatus using visuospatial working memory. Researchers have also implicated the visuospatial sketchpad in keeping track of changes in the visual perceptual world over time (Kahneman, Triesman, & Gibbs, 1992), maintaining orientation in space and directing spatial movement (Thomson, 1983), and comprehending certain types of verbal information (Mani & Johnson-Laird, 1982).

The central executive component of Baddeley's model is described as a limited-capacity mechanism responsible for coordinating tasks and managing the two slave systems. It operates in a fundamentally different way than the two slave systems, because it may be actively involved in meeting the demands of two or more concurrent tasks. Accordingly, performance declines only when the collective task demands exceed the capacity of resources.

Baddeley (1992) acknowledges that embarrassingly little direct research has focused on the central executive and that it is somewhat of a catch-all component responsible for a wide range of attentional duties. Nevertheless, one source of evidence derives from the study of Alzheimer's disease, a disorder typically associated with deficits in tasks believed to depend primarily on central executive functioning. In one study (Baddeley, 1993), Alzheimer's patients were trained to do a visual task and a verbal task. They then performed both tasks together in a dual-task paradigm. As the disease progressed, single task performance remained unchanged, but dual-task performance dropped markedly. This effect was interpreted as support for the modularity of the central executive, reasoning that time-sharing ability is accomplished entirely by the central executive

2.5 Working Memory in Writing

Kellogg (1996) proposed a model of writing that details how specific writing processes rely on the main components of Baddeley's working memory model. In this proposal, Kellogg distinguishes among three language production processes: formulating, executing, and monitoring. Each of these involves two basic level processes. Formulation consists of planning ideas and translating them into sentences that may later be hand written or typed. Execution includes programming (controlling motor movements) and executing (typing, handwriting, or dictation). Monitoring includes reading and editing. The model is very clear that writers do not necessarily progress serially from formulating text to executing it, and then to monitoring what they have written. Instead, the model supports simultaneous activation of each of these processes, provided that the demands placed on the central executive do not exceed its capacity limitations. Thus, the model anticipates that the typing of a word or phrase may take place simultaneously with the formulation of new material or reading previously written material. This is possible only when execution is well-practised and can proceed virtually automatically, so that central executive resources are not needed. In contrast, the basic processes of formulation and monitoring are much less likely to ever become automated.

Owing in part to its newness, little research has been reported that explicitly tests the implications of Kellogg's model.

2.6 An Adapted Working Memory Model

This section examines the assumptions of Baddeley's working memory model and proposes an adaptation that brings working memory into closer alignment with the attention literature, while simultaneously preserving its orientation toward complex language tasks. These adaptations to the working memory model have subtle implications for the dual-task methods for comparing visuospatial and verbal contributions to a primary task. Before addressing these methodological implications, however, a closer analysis of working memory is needed.

There are several interesting assumptions that are commonly made about the processing capabilities of the two slave systems. First, in comparisons of visuospatial and phonological loads, the structural assumption implies that the relative difficulty of the secondary tasks is irrelevant because any secondary task, regardless of difficulty, will engage the visuospatial sketchpad or phonological loop entirely, or not at all. Therefore, a phenomenologically easy visuospatial task, such as identifying in which ear a sound is played through headphones, should load the visuospatial sketchpad as much as a more difficult spatial task, such as mentally rotating a three dimensional object. If we assume, instead, that the slave systems represent pools of resources, then the difficulty of the secondary tasks becomes a variable of interest. This variable should be experimentally controlled because of the common finding that increasing the difficulty of a secondary task almost always results in a performance degradation in the primary task (Wickens, 1984; Navon & Gopher, 1979).

If we assume the slave systems are resource pools, then when we compare the relative effects of visuospatial and phonological load tasks on a primary task, it becomes important to equalize the overall difficulty of the loading tasks. Consider the implications of mistakenly assuming the slave systems are structures. If we disregard the difficulty of loading tasks, a disproportionately more difficult phonological task would disrupt the primary task of writing more than the visuospatial secondary task, possibly leading to the conclusion that the visuospatial sketchpad plays a smaller role in writing than it actually does. Thus, when comparing the contributions made by the two slave systems to a primary task under dual-task conditions, it may be more risky to assume that these components are structures rather than resource pools.

Another implication of Baddeley's theoretical assumptions is evident when comparisons are made of effects across studies. Under the assumption of structurally-based slave systems, differences in secondary task properties (including the frequency of response selection and execution as well as input and output modalities) will not affect the extent to which that task engages its targeted component. In contrast, resource allocation models assume that the frequency of response selection and the input and response modality are likely to affect the degree to which they interfere with a primary task. It is much easier to select secondary tasks if one adopts a structural assumption, but the results may be inaccurate if the visuospatial sketchpad and phonological loop are best conceptualized as pools of resources. As we discuss later, the criteria for specifying secondary tasks must be much more rigorous when a resource allocation model forms the theoretical framework.

Given these considerations, a new model of working memory is proposed that hypothesizes two mutually inaccessible pools of resources for verbal and visuospatial processing and storage. This model shares Friedman and Polson's (1981) concept of multiple resources, but differs because it includes Baddeley's idea of a limited capacity central executive system that is responsible for a wide range of attentional duties, including coordinating information between the visuospatial and verbal systems. Before developing the dual-task methods needed to investigate the relative contributions of visuospatial and phonological loop resources to writing, we sought in Experiment 1 to empirically validate the modified working memory model.

3 EXPERIMENT 1

If the phonological loop and visuospatial sketchpad of Baddeley's working memory model are engaged in a binary, all-or-none fashion, it follows that in a dual-task paradigm, secondary tasks of varying difficulty will have the same loading effect. This assumption is comparatively easy to test. For example, in a dual-task experiment, if two phonological secondary tasks of varying difficulty interfere equally with a primary task, then the all-or-none processing assumption is supported. Conversely, if the two phonological secondary tasks vary in the relative degree to which they disrupt primary task performance, then support tilts toward a capacity model in which resources are engaged in a graded fashion.

Baddeley's working memory model predicts no differences in performance related to type of irrelevant speech, because speech sounds, regardless of meaning, are believed to have obligatory access to the phonological store. Those sounds are believed to engage the phonological loop entirely due to its structural nature. Inconsistent with these predictions, Jones, Miles, and Page (1990) found that meaningful speech interfered more with the detection of spelling and typographical errors in a proof-reading task than the same speech played backward. However, in a second experiment, Jones et al. found no difference between the effect of reversed speech and a silent control on error detection rates, suggesting that reversed speech may not engage the phonological loop at all. It could be argued, however, that there may be so little phonemic similarity between forward and backward speech that it may not be reasonable to claim that speech played backward is really "speech." Further, Levy and Marek, elsewhere in this volume, report similar patterns of results in a writing study when computer-generated speech was "natural" and when the individual words in each sentence were randomly rearranged, but no changes made to their phonemic attributes. Their results may be limited by the writing task investigated. Rather than being "natural" essay writing, participants' memories were loaded with sets of words to use in formulating single sentences.

Our first experiment compares two types of irrelevant speech to test the hypothesis that the phonological loop can be differentially loaded in a dual-task paradigm. One recording was made of a passage read by the experimenter, and the other featured the same passage generated using a text-to-speech computer program. A structural model of the kind suggested by Baddeley predicts that accuracy on a primary memory task would be best in the absence of irrelevant speech. When either the human-generated or the computer-generated speech is delivered while participants perform another (primary) task, performance on the latter should decline, but the performance decrements should be similar for the two types of irrelevant speech. This would be so even if the materials delivered in a computer-synthesized speech generated a greater processing load (because it lacked nuances, had reduced inflections, and so forth) than the speech produced by a human voice. In contrast, our modified model, which anticipates such secondary tasks producing differential processing loads, would predict differential outcomes on the primary task.

3.1 Method

Participants
Twenty-six undergraduate students from the University of Florida participated in this experiment in partial fulfilment of a course requirement. Participants had neither impaired vision nor hearing.

Materials
Sets of five to nine randomly generated consonants were printed on transparencies presentation on an overhead projector. Consonant sets contained no duplicate letters, and no two sets were identical. Participants recorded their responses on printed answer sheets during the free recall phase of the experiment.

Two tapes of irrelevant speech were recorded. One featured a children's fable read by the experimenter. The other featured the same story generated via computer running a text-to-speech program. The content and acoustic energy level of the two taped presentations were the same.

Procedure
The to-be-remembered consonant sets were shown to the participants for 10 seconds each. Participants then had 20-seconds to recall the consonants. This sequence was repeated using 15 different sets of consonants for the baseline (no irrelevant speech) and each of the experimental conditions. During the experimental conditions, participants heard one of two types of irrelevant speech during the presentation portion of each trial. On alternate trials, the irrelevant speech was either human-generated or generated by computer.

3.2 Results and Discussion

The patterns shown in Figure 1 are compelling. For nearly all participants, the human-generated speech disrupted letter recall more than computer-generated speech, $F(1,23) = 33.85$, $p<.001$. These results parallel the participants' subjective reports that the computer-generated speech was easier to disregard. If the phonological loop is engaged in a binary fashion, the irrelevant computer-generated speech should be no more or less effective in disrupting a primary task than irrelevant human-generated speech. These results are more consistent with the hypothesis that the phonological loop is comprised of a pool of resources that can be engaged in a graded fashion. For convenience, we assume that the visuospatial sketchpad may also be considered as a resource pool, although its resources are allocated according to different rules to serve different functions.

If we can assume that the visuospatial sketchpad and the phonological loop represent pools of resources rather than structures, then it becomes important for researchers to agree on common criteria for selecting secondary tasks when their objective is to make comparisons between the effects of loading separate components of working memory. These considerations include the following:
- Secondary tasks should be equally demanding of attentional resources. Equivalency may be accomplished by comparing secondary task performance in isolation, or by placing each secondary task in a probe-tone paradigm in which subjects perform the load task as a primary task and are interrupted occasionally by a tone to which they respond as quickly as possible. Reaction times in probe tone paradigms are typically taken as an index of the mental effort demanded by the

primary task. More generally, any paradigm that enables the calculation of d', a measure of an observer's sensitivity to stimuli, will be satisfy this consideration.

- The loading tasks should not change in the degree to which they draw on controlled processes throughout the experiment. If a load becomes automated during the collection of data in a dual-task condition, then by the most common definitions of automaticity, it no longer draws on attentional resources. As a consequence, participants will work on the primary task as if they were working under single task conditions.
- The tasks should have similar structural composition, requiring the same mode of input and output.
- Response selection and execution should occur equally often in the tasks.
- Finally, secondary tasks should require different strategies for their successful performance. For example, a visuospatial task should not be easily performed by re-coding visuospatial stimuli into phonological stimuli. Thus, secondary tasks should be constructed so that performance differences will emerge if participants attempt to use the same strategies for each task.

Once appropriate secondary tasks are selected, the rationale for dual-task studies is relatively straightforward. By selectively engaging one component of working memory in a secondary task, the primary task then should draw only on the remaining resources. In Experiments 2 and 3, which incorporate the considerations we have just discussed, we investigate the contribution of visuospatial and verbal resources to writing in a dual-task paradigm.

Figure 1 *The effect of irrelevant speech type on recall of consonants as a function of memory set size.*

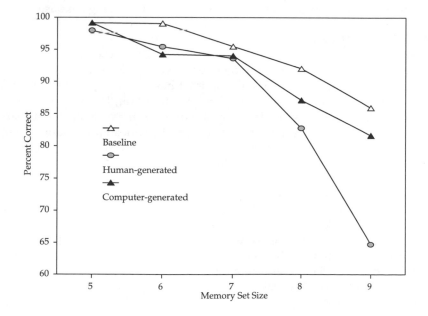

4   EXPERIMENT 2

The purpose of this experiment was to assess the contributions of the phonological loop to essay writing in a dual-task paradigm. Studies to date have addressed this issue by measuring writing quality and fluency in the presence and absence of irrelevant speech (Levy & Marek, this volume; Ransdell, Levy, & Kellogg, submitted). Because a major objective of this chapter was to compare the contributions of the phonological loop and the visuospatial sketchpad to writing, a new secondary task was needed. In particular, a task was needed which, unlike irrelevant speech, required measurable responses from the participant. Moreover, we sought a task that would enable us to present stimuli in this experiment and in Experiment 3 that were as similar as possible, yet would selectively engage the phonological loop and the visuospatial sketchpad, respectively. In each of these experiments, participants were made an explicit response whenever they detected a significant *visual* event. Sometimes this event occurred when this was their primary task. At other times, this event occurred while their primary task was composing an essay.

In the present experiment, the significant visual stimuli were very large single characters that alternated between alphabetical or numerical characters every 5 seconds. The participants' task was to signal whenever they detected the presentation of two alphabetic or two numerical characters in that occurred in succession, an event that occurred randomly, averaging twice each minute. In order to respond successfully, participants clearly had to categorize each stimulus (letter/digit), a task that should heavily involve the phonological loop as well as the central executive, but should involve the visuospatial sketchpad minimally, if at all.

4.1 Method

Participants
Forty-one University of Florida general psychology students participated in this study. All participants reported being proficient typists (mean typing speed = 32 wpm) and had experience interacting with a computer using a mouse.

Materials and Apparatus
Participants wrote essays on two open-ended topics, "The Perfect Job" and "The Greatest High." They used a Windows-based word processor written especially for this research effort. The program supported basic functions of text entry, cutting and pasting, and mouse control at the point of insertion. The program also enabled the presentation of the secondary task stimuli (directional symbols) in a large (120 pt) *sans serif* font displayed to the left of the text composition window. The characters subtended approximately 3 degrees of visual angle and were readily identifiable from the writers' peripheral vision.

Procedure
Participants first completed a 2-minute typing test in which they were asked to transcribe as quickly as possible the text that appeared on their screens. Next, they spent 20 minutes writing an essay on one of the two topics. Half wrote on "The Perfect Job," while the other half wrote about "The Greatest High." Participants were given notice 5 minutes before their time expired.

Participants next performed a phonological loop task as a single task for 5 minutes. This task was designed to load the phonological loop, but not the visuospatial sketchpad. During this task, a single letter or a single digit was shown for 5 seconds. At the end of this period, the visible stimulus was erased and replaced by another single character. The characters typically alternated between letters and digits. The participant's task was to indicate – by pressing the mouse button – whenever the category (letter or digit) remained the same from one presentation to the next (that is, two consecutive letters or numbers). Thus, if a letter was initially displayed, the participant made no response if it was replaced by a second (but different) letter, but responded if the second stimulus was a digit. A response was required, on the average, twice per minute. Consecutive letters and consecutive digits occurred equally often.

In the final, dual-task phase of the experiment, participants wrote for 20 minutes on whichever topic they had not already addressed earlier as the primary task. At the same time, they *simultaneously* performed the secondary loading task that they had just finished. Instructions for the loading task, stimuli presentation rate, and method of responding were identical to the single task conditions. Participants were instructed to perform both tasks to the best of their ability. To maintain interest in the task, the researcher promised that the person who performed the best overall would win $100.

4.2 Results and Discussion

Document quality was assessed on a 6-point scale using the essay-sort method by two independent raters (inter-rater reliability = 88%) (Madigan, Johnson, & Linton, 1994), and the number of words generated per minute measured document fluency. A signal detection paradigm (Green & Swets, 1966) was employed in the phonological secondary task. Signal detection is a well-established method used by engineers and by psychophysicists for estimating an observer's discriminative capacity or sensitivity to a signal independent of the observer's response bias. The measure of sensitivity is a pure number represented by the symbol, d'. Generally, the greater the value of d', the better the individual is able to correctly detect specific signals. In its specific details, the theory of signal detection requires a discussion of statistical concepts and topics that cannot be treated here.

As Table 1 indicates, performance in the present experiment deteriorated significantly from single to dual-task conditions on all measures. Words produced per minute dropped 21% (t (42) = 7.19, $p<.001$) and the quality of the essays declined 12.3% (t (42) = 2.71, $p=.01$) with the addition of the phonological loop secondary task. Most compelling was a 60% decrement in d' associated with the addition of the secondary task ($t(42) = 8.91$, $p <.001$).

5   EXPERIMENT 3

Because of the impressive amount of research on the effects of irrelevant speech on the variety of tasks discussed earlier, the focus of considerable recent work in writing has also focused on variables that might influence the engagement of the phonological loop (see, for example, Dansac & Passerault, 1998; Levy & Marek, in this volume; Ransdell, Levy, & Kellogg, in press). The role of visuospatial processing in writing has only received very little attention compared with the phonological loop (Dinet & Passerault, 1998; Levy, White, & Lea, 1998).

In the present experiment, we use the methodology underlying Experiment 2 to focus on how processing in the visuospatial sketchpad influences writing processes and products. Here, instead of monitoring digits and letters, participants monitored arrows that pointed up, down, left or right. They needed to form and remember a mental representation of the pattern that the arrows were tracing so that they could respond whenever a critical event occurred.

5.1 Method

Participants
A new group of 41 University of Florida general psychology students participated in this study. All participants reported to be proficient typists (mean typing speed = 32 wpm) and had experience interacting with a computer using a mouse.

Apparatus and Materials
The materials used in this experiment were identical to those used in Experiment 2.

Procedure
As in Experiment 2, participants first completed a 2-minute typing test in which they were asked to transcribe as quickly as possible text that appeared on their screens. Participants then wrote an essay for 20 minutes on one of the two topics used in Experiment 2

Participants next performed a visuospatial task for 5 minutes. This task was designed to load the visuospatial sketchpad but not the phonological loop. Rather than letters and digits, the computer displayed arrows were as large as the letters/digits in Experiment 2. The arrows pointed up, down, left, and right. The participants' task was to maintain in memory a representation of an x, y coordinate system and an imaginary placeholder at the 0,0 coordinate. They were to move the imaginary placeholder one standard, but arbitrary, unit of distance in the direction of the arrow presented. Any time the placeholder moved away from either axis and then returned to that axis they were to click the mouse. A new arrow was presented every 5 seconds and, on the average, a response was required twice per minute. Crossings of the x- and y-axis occurred equally often.

In the final, dual-task phase of the experiment, participants wrote for 20 minutes on whichever topic they had not already addressed earlier as the primary task. At the same time, they *simultaneously* performed the visuospatial loading task that they had just finished. Instructions for the loading task, stimuli presentation rate, and method of responding were identical to the single task conditions. Participants were instructed to perform both tasks to the best of their ability. To maintain interest in the task, the research promised that the person who performed the best overall would win $100.

5.2 Results and Discussion

Like Experiment 2, document quality was again assessed by two independent raters (inter-rater reliability = 84%) using the 6-point scale essay-sort method (Madigan, Johnson & Linton, 1994), document fluency was measured by the number of words generated per minute, and a signal detection paradigm (Green & Swets, 1966) was employed in the visuospatial secondary task.

The results indicated that, much like Experiment 2, performance in the present experiment deteriorated significantly from single to dual-task conditions on all measures. Words produced per minute declined 13% ($t(39) = 3.17$, $p<.01$) and the quality of the essays fell 13.6% (t (39) = 2.95, $p<.01$) with the addition of the phonological loop secondary task. A 44% decrement was observed in d' comparing single to dual-task conditions ($t(39) = 6.01$, $p <.001$).

6 COMBINED ANALYSIS OF EXPERIMENTS 1, 2, AND 3

Table 1   Mean d', writing speed, and writing quality scores for the single and dual visuospatial and phonological tasks. Standard errors in parentheses.

Measure	Visuospatial Single Task	Visuospatial Dual Task	Phonological Single Task	Phonological Dual Task
d'	3.50 (0.27)	1.96 (0.13)	4.09 (0.26)	1.64 (0.10)
Words per minute	14.7 (0.79)	12.8 (0.70)	16.2 (0.62)	12.8 (0.57)
Quality	3.16 (0.16)	2.73 (0.15)	3.18 (0.14)	2.79 (0.13)

As Table 1 shows, selectively engaging either component of working memory reliably slowed writing fluency, $F(1, 81) = 49.06$, $p <.001$. As Kellogg's model anticipates, there was a significant interaction between the component of working memory that was loaded and the testing conditions (either single or dual task), indicating that the phonological secondary task disrupted fluency more than the visuospatial secondary task, $F(1,81) = 3.99$, $p = .04$. Interestingly, the d' measured during the phonological secondary task declined much more than during the visuospatial sketchpad, as reflected in the interaction between loading task and the testing conditions, $F(1, 81) = 5.79$, $p < .01$. The decrement in d' associated with the dual task for the visuospatial group was 44%. For the phonological group, the d' fell 60%. Although quality was not affected more by one working memory load than another, both fluency and d' scores deteriorated more in the pairing of the phonological task with writing than in the pairing of the visuospatial task and writing. Despite the equal degradation in writing quality, these results suggest greater difficulty in timesharing writing with a phonological task than a with visuospatial task.

7 CONCLUSIONS

We believe that these findings support the recent trend toward multicomponent classes of working memory models, particularly those that distinguish between visuospatial and verbal/phonological processing. The data from Experiment 1 clearly present explanatory difficulties for classes of models, including Baddeley's, that postulate structures such as a phonological loop or a visuospatial sketchpad to operate as binary, all-or-none mechanisms. Instead, our data are compatible with an important, but seemingly subtle, variation that conceptualizes these mechanisms as pools of resources that can operate in a continuous or graded fashion. The distinction is important because it may help writing theorists and researchers to make closer contact with colleagues who are exploring other aspects of human cognitive processing, including speech production, language comprehension, or problem solving.

It is also clear from Experiments 2 and 3 that our data do not support the undifferentiated class of models that dominated early writing process research. Undifferentiated models would predict that equally demanding secondary tasks would be equally interfering with the writing primary task. Based on single task performance measures, our visuospatial and phonological tasks were statistically equivalent, although algebraically the visuospatial task was slightly more difficult as a single task. Nevertheless, when the loading tasks were performed at the same time that participants engaged in text production, the phonological task clearly interfered more than the visuospatial task.

We expect this line of research to extend to the subprocess level of writing, enabling investigations of the demands that formulating, executing and monitoring place on the visuospatial sketchpad and phonological loop. These future investigations will employ methods based on a resource capacity assumption of phonological loop and visuospatial sketchpad processing, and will include the methods for selecting secondary tasks that we addressed earlier.

Current research in our laboratory extends the methodologies introduced here to evaluate other claims from current working memory-based models of text production. For example, we have recently devised a way to overcome the inherent confounding in Experiments 2 and 3 between the specific stimuli shown and the participants' response decision rules by holding the stimuli constant. Thus, single alphabetic characters might be shown at the same rate as the stimuli presented before, but periodically they would simultaneously change colour, case, font, physical location, and value. Different groups of participants could be asked to respond whenever two stimuli in succession were the same colour or location (to engage the visuospatial sketchpad), or whenever the adjacent stimuli both contained a long "e" phoneme (to engage the phonological loop, or whenever they formed a 2-letter word (to focus on the central executive). The physical stimuli would remain the same, as would the physical response. Any difficulties between the single tasks or between their effects on the writing process would then simply be the result of the instructions designed to engage working memory components differentially.

AUTHOR NOTE

This chapter benefited greatly from the constructive suggestions made to earlier drafts by Ronald Kellogg. Correspondence concerning this chapter can be directed to C. Michael Levy, Department of Psychology, University of Florida, Box 112250, Gainesville FL USA 32611-2250 or by email to levy@ufl.edu.

REFERENCES

Atkinson, R.C., & Shiffrin, R.M.(1968). Human memory: A proposed system and its control processes. In K.W. Spence & J.T. Spence (Eds.), *The psychology of learning and motivation*: II. New York: Academic Press.

Baddeley, A. D., & Hitch, G.J. (1974). Working memory. In G. Bower (Ed.), *The psychology of learning and motivation, Vol. III*, pp. 47-90. New York: Academic Press.

Baddeley, A. D., Lewis, V., & Vallar, G. (1984). Exploring the articulatory loop. *The Quarterly Journal of Experimental Psychology, 36A*, 233-252.

Baddeley, A. D., Thomson, N., & Buchannon, M. (1975). Word length and the structure of short-term memory. *Journal of Verbal Learning and Verbal Behavior, 14*, 575-589.

Baddeley, A.D. (1993). Working memory or working attention? In A. Baddeley & L. Weiskrantz (Eds.). *Attention: Selection, Awareness & Control* (pp. 152-170). New York: Oxford.

Baddeley, A.D.(1992). Is working memory working? The fifteenth Bartlett lecture. *The Quarterly Journal of Experimental Psychology, 44a*, 1-31.

Baddeley, A.D., Papagno, C., & Vallar, G. (1988). When long-term learning depends on short-term storage. *Journal of Memory and Language, 27*, 586-595.

Bertelson, P. (1967). The psychological refractory period of choice reaction times with regular and irregular ISI's. *Acta Psychologica, 27*, 45-56.

Broadbent, D. (1958). *Perception and communication*. Oxford: Permagon.

Broadbent, D. (1982). Task communication and the selective intake of information. *Acta Psychologica, 50*, 253-290.

Brooks, L. R. (1968). Spatial and verbal components of the act of recall. *Canadian Journal of Psychology, 22*, 349-368.

Cherry, C. (1953). Some experiments on the recognition of speech with one and two ears. *Journal of the Acoustical Society of America, 23*, 915-919.

Craik, F. I. M., & Lockhart, F. S. (1972). Levels of processing: A framework for memory research. *Journal of Verbal Learning and Verbal Behavior, 11*, 671-684.

Craik, F. I. M., & Watkins, M. J. (1973). The role of rehearsal in short-term memory. *Journal of Verbal Learning and Verbal Behavior, 12*, 599-607.

Dansac, C., & Passerault, J. M. (1998, July). Disrupting central or phonological loop: Effects on the writing process and on the writing product. Paper presented at the *Writing98* Conference, Poitiers, France.

De Renzi, E., & Nichelli, P. (1975). Verbal and nonverbal short term memory impairment following hemispheric damage. *Cortex, 11*, 341-353.

Deutsch, F.A., & Deutsch, D. (1963). Attention: Some theoretical considerations. *Psychological Review, 70*, 80-90.

Dinet, J., & Passerault, J. J. (1998, July). Working memory and text production: The role of the visuospatial sketchpad in writing argumentative and descriptive texts. Paper presented at the *Writing98* Conference, Poitiers, France.

Fagot, C., & Pashler, H. (1992). Making two responses to a single object: Exploring the central attentional bottleneck. *Journal of Experimental Psychology: Human Perception and Performance, 18*, 1058-1079.

Frick, R. W. (1988). Issues of representation and limited capacity in the visuospatial sketchpad. *British Journal of Psychology, 79*, 289-308.

Friedman, A., & Polson, M. C. (1981). Hemispheres as independent resource systems: Limited-capacity processing and cerebral specialization. *Journal of Experimental Psychology: Human Perception and Performance, 7*, 1031-1058.

Gathercole, S., & Baddeley, A. D. (1992). *Working memory and language*. Hove, UK: Lawrence Erlbaum Associates.

Green, D., & Swets, J. (1966). *Signal detection theory and psychophysics*. New York: Wiley.

Henry, F. M. & Rogers, D. E. (1960). Increased response latency for complicated movements and a "memory drum" theory of neuromotor reaction. *Research Quarterly, 31*, 448-458.

Hue, C., & Ericson, J. R. (1988). Short-term memory for Chinese characters and radicals. *Memory & Cognition, 16*, 196-205.

Johnston, W.A., & Heinz, S.P. (1978). Flexibility and capacity demands of attention. *Journal of Experimental Psychology: General, 107*, 420-435.

Jones, D. M., Miles, C. & Page, J. (1990). Disruption of proof-reading by irrelevant speech: Effects of attention, arousal or memory? *Applied Cognitive Psychology, 4*, 89-108.

Kahenman, D., Triesman, A., & Gibbs, B. J. (1992). The reviewing of object files: Object specific integration of information. *Cognitive Psychology, 24*, 175-219.

Kahneman, D. (1973). *Attention and effort*. Englewood Cliffs, N.J.: Prentice-Hall.

Kantowitz, B. H. (1974). Double stimulation. In B. H. Kantowitz (Ed.), *Human information processing*. Hillsdale, NJ.: Lawrence Erlbaum Associates.

Kellogg, R. T. (1996). A model of working memory in writing. In C. M. Levy & S. Ransdell (Eds.) *The science of writing* (pp. 57-71). Mahwah, N.J.: Lawrence Erlbaum Associates.

Knowles, W. B. (1963). Operator loading tasks. *Human Factors, 5*, 151-161.

Levy, C. M., White, K., & Lea, J. (1998, July). The role of the visuospatial sketchpad in writing: Testing Kellogg's multicomponent model. Presented at the *Writing98* Conference, Poitiers, France.

Mackay, D.G. (1973). Aspects of the theory of comprehension, memory and attention. *Quarterly Journal of experimental Psychology, 25,* 22-40.

Madigan, R.J., Johnson, S.E., & Linton, P.W. (1994). Working memory capacity and the writing process. Paper presented at the American Psychological Society, Washington, D.C.

Mani, K., & Johnson-Laird, P.N. (1982). The mental representation of spatial descriptions, *Memory & Cognition, 10,* 181-187.

Moray, N. (1959). Attention in dichotic listening. *Quarterly Journal of Experimental Psychology, 11,* 56-60.

Moray, N. (1982). Subjective mental load. *Human Factors, 23,* 25-40.

Moray, N., Johannsen, G., Pew, R. W., Rasmussen, J., Sanders, A. F., & Wickens, C. D. (1979). Report of the experimental psychology group. In N. Moray (Ed.), *Mental workload: Its theory and measurement.* New York: Plenum.

Navon, D. (1984) Resources –A theoretical soup stone. *Psychological review, 91,* 216-234.

Navon, D., & Gopher, D. (1979). On the economy of the human-information processing system. *Psychological Review, 86,* 214-255.

Norman, D., & Bobrow, D. (1975). On data limited and resource limited processing. *Journal of Cognitive Psychology, 7,* 44-60.

Pashler, H. (1984). Processing stages in overlapping tasks: Evidence for a central bottleneck. *Journal of Experimental Psychology: Human Perception and Performance, 10,* 358-377.

Pashler, H., & Carrier, M. (1995). Attentional limits in memory retrieval. *Journal of Experimental Psychology: Learning Memory and Cognition, 21,* 1339-1348.

Pashler, H., & Johnston, J. C. (1989). Interference between temporally overlapping tasks: Chronometric evidence for ventral postponement with or without response grouping. *Quarterly Journal of Experimental Psychology, 41A,* 19-45.

Posner, M.I. and Boise, S.J. (1971). Components of attention. *Psychological Review, 78,* 391-49-408.

Ransdell, S., Levy, C. M., & Kellogg, R. T. (submitted). Concurrent loads on working memory during text production.

Rolfe, J.M. (1971). The secondary task as a measure of mental load. In W. T. Singleton, J.G. Fox & D. Whitfield (Eds.). *Measurement of man at work.* London: Taylor and Francis.

Salamé, P. & Baddeley, A. D. (1982b). Disruption of short-term memory by unattended speech: Implications for the structure of working memory. *Journal of Verbal Learning and Verbal Behavior, 21,* 150-164.

Salamé, P., & Baddeley, A. D. (1982a). Effects of background music on phonological short-term memory. *Quarterly Journal of Experimental Psychology, 41A,* 107-122.

Shallice, T., & Warrington, E. K. (1970). Independent functioning of verbal memory stores: A neuropsychological study. *Quarterly Journal of Experimental Psychology, 22,* 261-273.

Sternberg, S. (1969). The discovery of processing stages: Extensions of Donders' method. *Acta Psychologica, 30,* 276-315.

Thomson, J. A. (1983). Is continuous visual monitoring really necessary in visually guided locomotion? *Journal of Experimental Psychology: Human Perception and Performance. 9,* 427-443.

Triesman, A. M., & Davies, A. (1973). Divided attention to ear and eye. In S. Kornblum (Ed.). *Attention and performance* (Vol. 4). New York: Academic Press.

Tulving, E. (1966). Subjective organization and effects of repetition in multi-trial free-recall learning. *Journal of Verbal Learning and Verbal Behavior, 6,* 193-197.

Tzeng, O.J. (1973). Positive recency effects in delayed free recall. *Journal of Verbal Learning and Verbal Behavior, 12,* 436-439.

Vallar, G., & Baddeley, A. D. (1984). Fractionation of working memory. Neuropsychological evidence for a phonological short-term store. *Journal of Verbal Learning and Verbal Behavior, 23,* 151-161.

Welford, A. T. (1967). Single channel operations in the brain. *Acta Psychologica, 27,* 5-22.

Wickens, C. D. (1984). Processing resources in attention. In R. Parasuraman, (Ed.). *Varieties of attention.* New York: Academic Press.

Subject - verb agreement errors in writing: phonological and semantic control in adults

Isabelle Negro
   L.E.A.D./C.N.R.S., Université de Bourgogne, France
Lucile Chanquoy
   Université Paul Valéry, Montpellier, France

ABSTRACT

This work was designed to study subject-verb agreement errors. These errors occur rarely but regularly even in the writing of highly educated adults. In two experiments, twenty adults were orally presented with sentences to write. The sentences were in the French present or past indicative (the imperfect tense) and were constructed as follows: Article + Noun 1 + Preposition + Noun 2 + Verb + Adverbial Phrase. Noun 1 and Noun 2 always mismatched in number. In the first experiment, phonological information provided by the subject noun was manipulated. In the second experiment, preverbal nouns and adverbial phrases were manipulated in order to control semantic information. Results showed that adults made more errors with irregular and pseudo-plural nouns than with regular nouns with the present tense (Experiment 1). Conversely, adults made more errors with plausible local nouns only with the imperfect tense (Experiment 2). Globally, results showed that the ratio of errors increased when no semantic or phonological information was available.

1   INTRODUCTION

Written production is a complex activity composed of at least three main systems: formulation, execution and monitoring (Kellogg, 1996). Each of these three systems involves two processes. To formulate, the writer must set goals, retrieve relevant ideas from long term memory, and organize these ideas into a global plan (planning). The writer must then translate these ideas into syntactically and lexically correct sentences (translating). The output of translation is executed by the handwriting or typing process using programming and executing processes. Finally, the monitoring system reads the whole text (reading) and compares the initial goals with the written production (editing).

The new and fundamental element of Kellogg's model is the main role of the monitoring system. This model does not mean that the writer formulates, executes, and then checks a text. On the contrary, simultaneous activation of these different processes can be possible, controlled by the monitoring system, and this activation can occur before or during the production of handwritten text. During formulation the writer activates some semantic, syntactic, phonological, and orthographic subprocesses to translate an idea into a written message. According to Kellogg (1996), the writer is able to listen to already produced sentences as " internal speech " (Vygotsky, 1962) or a " pre-text " (Witte & Cherry, 1994) before their graphic execution. Thus, the reading and editing processes can appear once the text is entirely written or before the final output. The existence of such a control was found by Levelt (1989) in oral production and called pre-articulatory control. If this control system exists, as has been described by Kellogg and Levelt, it is plausible to think that writers are able to correct a certain number of errors before their graphic realization. Here we focus on orthographic errors, and more particularly on subject-verb agreement errors.

These kinds of errors usually appear in spontaneous productions when three principal features are present (Fayol & Got, 1991):

a   two nouns or pronouns belonging to the same phrase are plausible subjects of the same verb (for example: " the horses of the soldier are running in the field ");

b   these two nouns or pronouns differ in number (*i.e.*, singular-plural or plural-singular);

c   the difference in number is not orally pronounced (in French: *L'oiseau chante / Les oiseaux chantent* [the bird sings / The birds sing]).

Thus these errors mainly consist of making the verb agree with the noun that immediately precedes it, instead of with its subject, a phenomenon that is referred to as a proximity concord error (Francis, 1986).

At the beginning of the 1990s, the hypothesis that subject-verb agreement errors were caused by a temporary cognitive overload in working memory was prominent, especially in French research about writing (Fayol & Got, 1991; Fayol, Largy, & Lemaire, 1994; Negro, Chanquoy, & Fayol, 1994). This hypothesis was tested using the dual task paradigm. Writers had to write down sentences and, for example, simultaneously retain and subsequently recall a list of words. Results showed that subjects made more errors when they had to recall both the sentences and the series of words (extra cognitive load). These experiments were led with verbs conjugated in the present indicative. However, these results have not been replicated with verbs conjugated in the imperfect or future tenses (*cf.* for example, Chanquoy & Negro, 1996a). In addition, according to Bock and Cutting (1992) and Bock and Miller (1991), the hypothesis concerning a temporary cognitive overload cannot be accepted, at least for oral language. These authors have indeed shown in several experiments that an increase in the length of a phrase between the subject noun and the verb (that could be considered as an extra load) did not result in an increase in the proportion of agreement errors. A replication of Bock's experiments in French written language showed the same pattern of results (Chanquoy & Negro, 1996b; Negro & Chanquoy, 1997).

Consequently, due to these conflicting results and to Kellogg's new model, part of the research is currently focused on the existence of a pre-graphic control that would consume more or less cognitive resources according to the amount of available phonological and/or semantic information. American, Italian, and French researchers are currently interested in phonological and semantic controls on subject-verb agreement errors (See, for example, Bock & Cutting, 1992; Hupet, Fayol, & Schelstraete, 1998; Largy, 1995; Vigliocco, Butterworth, & Semenza, 1995). Before presenting some of their results, a model of agreement is proposed.

Fayol, Hupet, Largy and Schelstraete (submitted) have built a two-step model for subject-verb agreement. During the first step, the number of the verb would be automatically activated by the number of the closest noun (for example, " The dog belonging to the children *bark* " [instead of *barks*]). During the second step an editing control, similar to the monitoring process (Kellogg, 1996; Levelt, 1989) would be implemented each time a morphological ambiguity is perceived, and particularly when there are two preverbal nouns that differ in number (Singular-Plural or Plural-Singular; Hupet, Schelstraete, Demaeght & Fayol, 1996). Therefore, under these particular conditions, a possibility of control on a phonological level and/or at a semantic level could exist for Singular-Plural and Plural-Singular conditions.

In addition, the analysis of adults' spontaneous productions reveals that expert writers make few or no agreement errors when the verbal end is orally marked (Fayol & Got, 1991). However, experiments in French show that errors appear when verbal morphemes are written but not orally pronounced (for example: *il chante / ils chantent* [he sings / they sing] vs *il boit / ils boivent* [he drinks / they drink]). These results indicate the importance of phonological control during the writing process (for example: Negro & Chanquoy, submitted).

The hypothesis relative to the impact of phonological factors has already been shown by Berko (1958) and Stemberger (1983) for the morphology of words, and especially the morphology of subject nouns. These authors have shown that English speakers do not add plural marks with nouns ending in /s/ or /z/ sounds, that is, with nouns that already have plural morphology. In French, Largy (1995) conducted an experiment about subject-verb agreement. In his work, writers were asked to write down, using the present tense, orally presented sentences conjugated with the French imperfect tense. Sentences were structured as follows: " Noun 1 belonging to Noun 2 + Verb ". Verbs belong to the first indicative group or to another group. With the imperfect, the difference between the third singular person and the third plural person is not orally marked whatever the verbal group. Conversely, with the present, only the French first group verbs keep the phonetic ambiguity. Results showed that the phonological information presented *via* the verbal flexion decreased agreement errors. It seems that this information has allowed writers to detect eventual errors when the two nouns were different in number, and therefore they were able to choose the appropriate morpheme. An ambiguity of the verbal morphology would be better detected when there is pre-graphic phonological control. This control would be possible through the phonological loop, in working memory (Baddeley, 1986, 1990; Baddeley & Hitch, 1974).

Thus there seems to be both theoretical and empirical support for pre-graphic and pre-articulatory phonological control processes. Nevertheless, some English studies do not validate this hypothesis. Bock and Cutting (1992) and Bock and Miller (1991) asked English speakers to continue subject phrases as 'Noun 1 + Noun 2' (for example: " The key to the cabinets ") in order to make complete sentences. Most of the speakers ended the sentences using the verb 'to be'. In English, as in French, the verbal flexion of the third person for this verb is phonologically different for the singular and for the plural. However, participants made subject-verb agreement errors.

These different experiments focused mainly on the phonological information brought on by the verbal flexion. However only Bock and Eberhard (1993) studied the impact of the phonology of preverbal nouns (i.e., local nouns that are the second noun in sentences built as 'Noun1 + Noun 2 + Verb) on the agreement. These authors asked speakers to continue preambles, where the head noun (the subject of the verb) was always singular and the local noun was either a pseudo-plural (singular noun with a plural phonology: 'course'), a singular ('court'), or a true plural ('courts'). Contrary to their hypotheses, results showed no effect of phonology. For example, subjects did not make any errors with pseudo-plural nouns while they made many errors with true plural local nouns. The lack of effect could be explained by the fact that these authors have studied the phonological effect only on local nouns. However, verbal agreement is built from the subject of the verb. It would therefore be more interesting to study the subject noun instead of the local noun phonology.

Vigliocco, Butterworth and Semenza (1995) were also interested in this issue. They proposed a completion task to Italian speakers, and they manipulated head nouns (subjects). There were regular nouns (singular: *gatto* / plural: *gatti*), invariable nouns (*città*), or collective nouns (singular: *illustrazione* / plural: *illustrazioni*). In Italian, collective nouns are morpho-phonologically ambiguous because the singular with '*e*' corresponds to plural feminine nouns (*la ragazza* / *le ragazze*), and the plural with '*i*' corresponds to plural masculine nouns (*il gatto* / *i gatti*). Results showed that Italian speakers made more errors with invariable nouns than with ambiguous collective nouns or regular nouns. The number of subject-verb agreement errors significantly increased when there were no phonological clues. Conversely, the number of errors did not significantly increase with ambiguous collective nouns. It seems that speakers tried to understand the meaning of the sentence 'on-line'. Speakers and probably writers too would use semantic clues to avoid subject - verb agreement errors, mainly when the task is not too resource consuming. Thus it is possible to consider two kinds of pre-articulatory or pre-graphic control: a phonological one, and a semantic one. This means that the monitoring system could be warned either by phonological or semantic information during formulation, recall or completion of sentences.

Bock and Miller (1991) studied the semantic variable by manipulating the animate or inanimate characteristics of local nouns (Noun 2). According to these authors, in our daily discourse the head noun is more often animate than inanimate. Thus speakers would make errors with an inanimate head noun combined with an animate local noun. However, no significant results were found, and they concluded that semantic clues had no effect on agreement errors. Bock and Eberhard (1993) also compared the effect on agreement errors of collective nouns (for example: the police) and non collective nouns (the policeman). Their hypothesis predicted that collective nouns would systematically lead to plural verbal flexions. However, no significant differences between collective and non collective nouns were observed.

These last few studies were all with English speakers, and because each language has its own idiosyncrasies (Goodluck & Häkansson, 1984) it is possible to predict different results in French. In addition, these studies were primarily interested in the semantic characteristics of local nouns. Nevertheless, while studying semantic clues, it seems important to take into account the general meaning of the sentence. French researchers studied this aspect in written productions. Largy (1995) analyzed the homophony between a noun and a verb (for example, in French: *la porte* [the door] / *il porte* [he wears]). Sentences that preferentially activate nominal (*Le menuisier ponce les fenêtres, il les porte* [The carpenter sands down the windows, he carries them]) or verbal candidates (*L'esclave soulève les fardeaux, il les porte* [The slave lifts the burdens, he carries them]) were orally dictated to participants who had to write them down. The frequency of verbal and nominal candidates was equally manipulated. Results showed that writers made more errors with verbs having nominal homophones. They also made more errors when the frequency of the noun was higher than the verbal frequency (Largy, Fayol & Lemaire, 1996). However, if writers really interpreted sentences, they would not confuse a verb with a noun. These confusions would not result from the meaning associated with the sentence (of course adult participants understood these sentences), but from a syntactic attraction phenomenon between the pronoun *les* (them), that can also be an article (the) and the verb, that can be here confused with a noun.

With another kind of procedure, Fayol, Hupet, Largy and Schelstraete (submitted) and Hupet, Schelstraete, Demaeght and Fayol (1996) have equally shown a semantic effect. They asked writers to recall sentences either presented in a conventional order (Subject + Verb + Complement: SVC) or inverted (Complement + Verb + Subject: CVS). The complement and the subject noun were two semantically plausible subjects for the verb (SVC: *Le marin chante avec ses amis* [The sailor sings with his friends]), or only the head noun was plausible (CVS: *Pendant la récréation, chante les enfants* [literally: During playtime, sing children]). The agreement errors were more numerous with inverted sentences and plausible complements. The major problem of the study is that even in French inverted sentences are rare in spontaneous production. Therefore it is impossible to determine if the increase in errors is due to the manipulated semantic factor or to the scattered numbers of this syntactic structure.

The objective of the following studies was to see if phonological or semantic information was used by the monitoring system (Kellogg, 1996) to control and to correct subject-verb agreement errors, before the graphic execution of sentences. Taking into account the results formulated from the preceding experiments, the effects of the phonological characteristics of head nouns and the semantic information conveyed by the sentence were analyzed. In addition, studies in English, Italian or French have mainly focused on agreements of verbs in the present indicative. Here, a comparison between the present and the past indicative in adult expert writers was examined. Thus, these experiments were designed to explore the processing underlying verb-number agreement in French, focusing on the contribution of phonological and semantic factors. The first question was whether the phonology of the plural supported agreement. The second question examined the effect of semantic clues on agreement.

2   EXPERIMENT 1: PHONOLOGICAL CONTROL

2.1 Hypotheses

To study the effect of phonological characteristics on subject-verb agreement errors, three categories of head nouns were manipulated: regular nouns, irregular nouns and pseudo-plural nouns. Irregular nouns have phonologically irregular plurals (*cheval - chevaux* [horse - horses]). Pseudo-plural nouns are phonologically closer to plural irregular nouns (*pruneau - pruneaux* [prune - prunes]).

We tested four hypotheses.

First, the tense would not modify the ratio of agreement errors. Participants would make a relatively stable ratio of errors for the present and for the imperfect (*Cf.* Chanquoy & Negro, 1996a & b; Negro & Chanquoy, 1995, 1996). The tenses were manipulated because children participated equally in this experiment (and the following one). For these participants, we expected a tense effect that is not developed here.

We expected an effect of the nature of the local noun on the ratio of errors. Participants would make fewer agreement errors with irregular nouns because they would systematically use the correct verbal ending, due to oral clues provided in pronouncing these irregular nouns. Conversely, the ratio of errors would increase without phonological information, with regular nouns whose endings are not marked.

Second, the ratio of errors would be more prevalent with pseudo-plural nouns which lead to phonological ambiguities. There would be more errors when the head noun is phonologically close to an irregular plural (ending in the same sound /o/, i.e., for the singular: *pruneau* [prune] and for the plural: *pruneaux* [prunes]).

Third, the number of head and local nouns would have an effect on the ratio of errors. According to Bock and Cutting (1992) and Bock and Miller (1991), a plural local noun leads to more errors than a singular local noun. Thus, more errors in Singular-Plural conditions than in Plural-Singular conditions are expected. Bock and Miller (1991) for oral language, and Fayol, Largy, and Lemaire (1994) for written language have both shown that agreement errors are significantly more frequent when the subject noun is singular and the local noun is plural. The singular form is more frequent in all languages, thus a singular head noun could lead to the corresponding singular inflection by automatic location of the subject of the verb. However, this pattern of results has not been obtained in experiments using imperfect indicative (Chanquoy & Negro, 1996a).

Finally, if the Singular-Plural condition is more complex than the Plural-Singular condition due to the plural local noun, and if pseudo-plural nouns lead to more errors than regular and irregular nouns, then the ratio of agreement errors would dramatically increase in the Singular-Plural condition, especially when the head noun is pseudo-plural.

2.2 Method

Participants

Forty students participated in this experiment (mean age 21.1 years, ranging from 19.2 to 31.6). They were all French native speakers.

Materials

The stimuli were 6 filler sentences and 12 experimental sentences. These sentences were constructed as follows: Article (1 syllable) + Noun 1 (2 syllables) + Preposition (1 syllable) + Noun 2 (2 syllables) + Verb (2 syllables) + Adverbial Phrase (4 syllables).

The objective of the adverbial phrase was to lengthen the sentence and its position was not manipulated unlike the procedure in the study by Largy, Chanquoy and Fayol (1993).

The first noun was always the subject of the verb and had different phonological characteristics: regular plural, irregular plural or pseudo-plural. Among the 12 target sentences, four sentences had irregular subjects (*Le signal des avions avance dans le ciel bleu* [The signal behind planes advance in the blue sky]), four had pseudo-plural nouns (*Les pruneaux du dessert brûlent dans le four* [The prunes on the cake burn in the oven]), and four had regular nouns (*Les camoins du patron glissent sur la chaussée* [The trucks of the boss slip on the pavement]). In translating these examples we have retained French syntax.

The head and the local nouns always differed in number: singular head noun and plural local noun (Singular-Plural) or plural head noun and singular local noun (Plural-Singular).

The verbs of experimental and filler sentences were conjugated either with the present or the imperfect indicative in accordance with the writing groups. Present tense sentences were the same as imperfect sentences since they were not proposed to the same writers. Finally, each writer had a booklet to recall the orally presented sentences (one sentence per page).

Procedure
The 40 participants were divided into two groups of 20 subjects. The first group dealt with the sentences conjugated in the present and the second group with sentences conjugated in the imperfect. The participants were divided into small groups. For each group, the sentences were not presented in the same order to avoid a possible order effect. They were informed then that they would hear sentences which they had to write down as quickly as possible. The sentences were recorded on an audio-tape to control the speaking rate.

For each trial the experimenter played a single sentence (either filler or experimental), and then paused the audio-tape. This cued the participants to write down the sentence, then immediately turn the page of the booklet, and wait for another sentence. Neither revision nor correction was allowed. Previous instructions specified that the purpose of the experiment was to study the memorization of sentences.

Design and data analysis
The dependent variable was the mean ratio of agreement errors (*i.e.*, the number of subject-verb agreement errors divided by the number of acceptable sentences). This ratio was computed for each participant in each condition. The data were analyzed with a 2 [Verbal Tense: present or imperfect] x 3 [Type of subject: irregular, pseudo-plural, or regular] x 2 [Number of preverbal nouns: Singular-Plural or Plural-Singular] analysis of variance with repeated measures on the last two factors.

In addition, we performed an ANOVA with the sentence items as random factor (F2). For clarity, only the results with the participants as random factor are presented here.

2.3 Results

The mean ratio of agreement errors is shown in Table 1.

Table 1   *Mean ratios of subject-verb agreement errors as a function of the nature of the subject noun (irregular, pseudo-plural, or regular), the number of the preverbal nouns (Singular-Plural or Plural-Singular), and the tenses (present or imperfect).*

	Irregular		Pseudo-plural		Regular	
	Singular-Plural	Plural-Singular	Singular-Plural	Plural-Singular	Singular-Plural	Plural-Singular
Present	.175	.10	.25	.075	.050	.075
Imperfect	.075	0	.175	.025	.075	.10

The results showed that, as expected, the ratio of agreement errors did not significantly vary between the present and the imperfect (.12 and .08; $F(1,38) = 1.14$, NS).

Figure 1   *Mean ratios of agreement errors associated with number of head and local nouns, and with the head noun's phonological characteristics, in sentences with verbs conjugated in the present.*

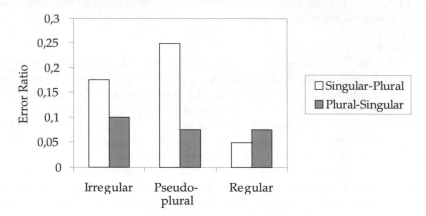

The analysis relative to each verbal tense showed that, for verbs in the present tense writers tended to make more errors with irregular (.14) and pseudo-plural (.16) head nouns rather than with regular nouns (.06; $F(2,38) = 2.55$, $p < .09$). There was no effect for the number of head and local nouns (Singular-Plural = .16, Plural-Singular = .08; $F(1,19) = 2.34$, NS). The interaction among the types of head nouns and the number of head and local nouns was not significant ($F(2,38) = 2.33$, NS). Nevertheless, the planned comparison opposing the most difficult condition (pseudo-plural head noun and Singular-Plural) to all the others was significant ($F(1,38) = 9.19$, $p < .005$; See Figure 1).

However, for imperfect verbs differences among noun conditions were not significant (regular = .09, irregular = .09, pseudo-plural = .1; $F(2,38) = 1.25$, NS). The number of head and local nouns had no significant effect on the ratio of errors (Sin-

Figure 2   *Mean ratios of agreement errors associated with number and characteristics of head nouns, and number of local nouns, with the imperfect tense.*

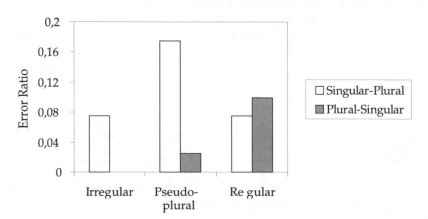

gular-Plural = .10, Plural-Singular = .04; F(1,19) = 1.97, NS). Finally, the interaction between type of head noun and number of preverbal nouns approached significance (F(2,38) = 3.15, p < .06). With irregular and pseudo-plural nouns, errors appeared mainly in singular-plural conditions, whereas with regular nouns, there were the same proportions of errors in singular-plural and plural-singular conditions. The planned comparison opposing a pseudo-plural singular head noun combined with a plural local noun to all the other conditions was significant (F(1,38) = 8.53, p < .006; see Figure 2).

2.4 Discussion

The hypothesis that predicted no tense effect was confirmed. The adults made approximately the same number of errors with the present and imperfect indicative (Chanquoy & Negro, 1996a). With the types of head nouns the results were partially consistent with our hypothesis. Regular nouns led to fewer errors than pseudo-plural nouns, but even fewer than with irregular nouns. However, this effect was only significant for the present tense. Thus, if writers used phonological characteristics provided by the head nouns, irregular nouns would lead to significantly fewer errors than regular and pseudo-plural nouns. This result showed that phonological information brought by the head noun did not allow writers to correct agreement errors before writing.

Contrary to our hypothesis and to Bock and Miller's (1991) and Bock and Cutting's (1992) results, agreement errors were not significantly more frequent when the head noun was singular and the local noun was plural, whatever the verbal tense. Even if participants made more errors in Singular-Plural conditions for both tenses, this difference never achieved significance. Moreover, the hypothesis that predicted an interaction among the type of head nouns and the number of local and head nouns was not confirmed. This interaction was found only in the imperfect condition. However, the planned comparison opposing a pseudo-plural head noun combined with a plural local noun to all the other conditions was significant for the two verbal tenses. A pseudo-plural singular head noun in Singular-Plural condition led to an ambiguity with the verbal agreement, and led to a greater number of errors. Opposed to Vigliocco, Butterworth and Semenza (1995), the phonological characteristics of subject nouns were not sufficient to warn the pre-graphic control system (Kellogg, 1996; Levelt, 1989), and avoid possible agreement errors. A phonological ambiguity (pseudo-plural) associated with a plural local noun (Singular-Plural) would prevent the pre-graphic control probably because too many cognitive resources would be used to try to solve the ambiguity of head nouns.

As a result, these findings were not entirely consistent with a phonological contribution to agreement control and with our hypothesis about the influence of phonology on agreement errors.

3   EXPERIMENT 2: SEMANTIC CONTROL

The general objective of the second study was to analyze the effect of semantic factors on the ratio of agreement errors. The experimental sentences used here were different than those used by Fayol, Hupet, Largy and Schelstraete (submitted). They were syntactically more frequent (*e.g.*, canonical order of the words), and did not contain any ambiguity between nouns and verbs (contrary to Largy, 1995).

Adult writers were asked to recall sentences built as follows: " Noun 1 belong-ing to Noun 2 + Verb + Adverbial Phrase ". Half the sentences had a local noun (Noun 2) that was a semantically plausible subject of the verb, and the other half had a non plausible local noun. An adverbial phrase was added at the end of each sentence. This phrase was either a neutral adverb that did not provide any semantic information, or a present participle that added semantic information by reinforcing the plausibility of the head noun.

3.1 Hypotheses

To analyse the effect of semantic characteristics, two categories of local nouns (plau-sible and non plausible), and two categories of adverbial phrases (providing or not providing semantic information reinforcing the head noun) were manipulated.

We tested four hypotheses: First, as in the previous experiment, we predicted that for adult participants the tense would not modify the ratio of agreement errors (cf. Chanquoy & Negro, 1996a & b). Second we predicted an effect of the nature of the local noun on the ratio of errors. The ratio of errors would increase when local nouns were plausible subjects of the verb. Thus, when the local noun is plausible, the monitoring system cannot use semantic information to prevent errors since the two preverbal nouns are plausible subjects of the same verb. In this particular case, proximity errors would be numerous. Third, we predicted that adults would make more agreement errors with neutral adverbs than with present participles. If the adverbial phrase especially referred to the head noun, rather than to the local noun the control system could be alerted and the erroneous verbal flexion would be cor-rected. Fourth, concerning the number of head and local nouns, two concurrent hypotheses were tested. According to Bock and Miller (1991) or Bock and Cutting (1992), a plural local noun led to more errors than a singular local noun. However, this effect was not found in the first experiment with French writers.

Finally, the ratio of errors should increase when the local noun is plausible and when the adverbial phrase is an adverb, that is, without any semantic information. In addition, if the Singular-Plural condition is more difficult than the Plural-Singu-lar condition, we expected that adults would make more errors with a plural plau-sible local noun and an adverb than in the other conditions.

3.2 Method

Participants
Forty students took part in this experiment (mean age 22.1 years, ranging from 18.6 to 33.5). None of the students had participated in the first experiment and they were all French native speakers.

Materials
The experimental materials consisted of 8 filler sentences and 16 experimental sen-tences. These sentences were constructed as follows: Article (1 syllable) + Noun 1 (2 syllables) + Preposition (1 syllable) + Noun 2 (2 syllables) + Verb (2 syllables) + Adverbial Phrase (4 syllables). Noun 1 and Noun 2 systematically differed in number: singular Noun 1 and plural Noun 2 (Singular-Plural) or plural Noun 1 and singular Noun 2 (Plural-Singular).

The adverbial phrase was either a present participle reinforcing the meaning of the sentence and characterizing the subject of the verb (head noun), or a neutral adverb that just specified the verb.

Some sentences are given for example:

- Plausible local noun (Noun 2) with a present participle, Singular-Plural condition: *Le chat des enfants gratte en miaulant* (The cat belonging to the children scratches while mewing);
- Non plausible local noun, with an adverb, Plural-Singular condition: *Les loups de la forêt hurlent violemment* (The wolfs in the forest howl violently).

Among the 16 experimental sentences, eight sentences had plausible head and local nouns, and eight sentences had only plausible head nouns. For each of these eight sentences, four were presented with a present participle and four with a neutral adverb. Finally, among these four sentences, two had a singular head noun and a plural local noun (Singular-Plural), and two had a plural head noun and a singular local noun (Plural-Singular). The verbs of experimental and filler sentences were conjugated either with the present or with the imperfect indicative in accordance with the writing groups. The sentences were the same for the two tenses since they were not proposed to the same writers. Finally, each writer had a booklet to recall the orally presented sentences.

Procedure

The procedure and the instructions used for this experiment were identical to those used in the first experiment.

Design and data analysis: The mean ratio of agreement errors was analyzed with a 2 [Verbal Tense: present or imperfect] x 2 [Plausibility of Noun 2: plausible or non plausible] x 2 [Nature of the adverbial phrase: adverb or present participle] x 2 [Number of preverbal nouns: Singular-Plural or Plural-Singular] analysis of variance with repeated measures on the last three factors.

We equally performed an ANOVA with the sentence items as random factor (F2). The obtained results were the same. Thus for clarity, only the results with the participants as random factor are presented here.

3.3 Results

Table 2 shows that the ratio of agreement errors did not significantly vary between the present and the imperfect (.05 and .03; $F(1,19) = 1.28$, NS).

Table 2   *Mean ratios of subject-verb agreement errors as a function of the nature of the plausibility of the local noun (plausible or non plausible), the nature of the complement (present participle vs adverb), the number of the preverbal nouns (Singular-Plural or Plural-Singular), and the tenses (present or imperfect).*

| | Plausible | | | | Non Plausible | | | |
| | Present participle | | Adverb | | Present Participle | | Adverb | |
	Sing-Plur	Plur-Sing	Sing-Plur	Plur-Sing	Sing-Plur	Plur-Sing	Sing-Plur	Plur-Sing
Present	.050	0	.20	0	.075	.025	.025	.050
Imperfect	.025	.025	.125	.025	0	0	0	.025

Figure 3   *Present tense: Mean ratios of agreement errors associated with number of nouns,*
              semantic characteristics (plausibility [Plaus.] or non plausibility [Non Plaus.] of
              local nouns [N2]), and nature of the complement (present participle [P.Part.] or
              adverb [Adv.]).

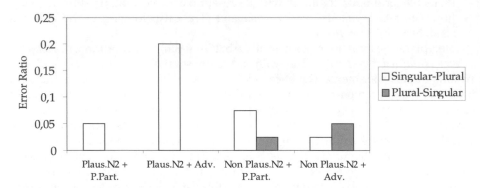

For the present, writers made significantly more errors in Singular-Plural conditions than in Plural-Singular conditions (.09 *vs.* .02; F(1,19) = 5.01, p < .04). Conversely, the ratio of errors did not vary with the plausibility of the local noun (plausible: .06 and non plausible: .04; F(1,19) < 1), and with the nature of the adverbial
phrase (present participle: .04 and adverb: .07; F(1,19) = 2.02 NS). The interaction
among the number of preverbal nouns, the plausibility of local nouns and the nature of the adverbial phrase was nearly significant (F(1,19) = 3.67, p < .07). The
planned comparison opposing the most difficult condition (plausible Noun 2, adverb and Singular-Plural condition) to all the others was also significant (F(1,19) =
14.31, p < .001; see Figure 3).

For imperfect verbs the number of head and local nouns had no effect on the
ratio of errors (Singular-Plural = .04, Plural-Singular = .02; F(1,19) = 1.88, NS). Participants made significantly more errors when the local noun was a plausible subject for the verb (.05 *vs.* .01; F(1,19) = 4.41, p < .05). In addition, the presence of a
neutral adverb led to more errors than a present participle (.05 *vs.* .01; F(1,19) = 6.33,

Figure 4   *Imperfect tense: Mean ratios of agreement errors associated with number of*
              nouns, semantic characteristics, and nature of the complement.

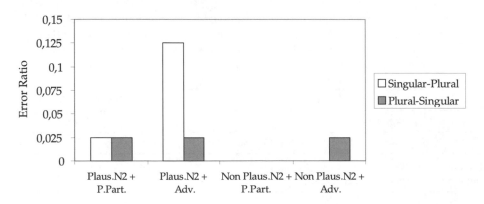

p <.02). Finally, the interaction among the number of preverbal nouns, the plausibility of local nouns, and the nature of adverbial phrase was significant $(F(1,19) = 6.33$, $p < .02)$. The planned comparison opposing sentences with a singular plausible local noun and an adverb to others was also significant $(F(1,19) = 34.78, p < .001$; see Figure 4).

3.4 Discussion

Once again, the hypothesis that predicted no tense effect was confirmed. Adults were able to make a verb agree when it was conjugated either in the present or imperfect indicative.

The second hypothesis was that plausible local nouns would lead to more errors than non plausible local nouns. This hypothesis was only confirmed with the imperfect indicative.

Concerning the nature of the adverbial phrase, the results partially confirmed our hypothesis. Adults made more errors with a neutral adverb than with a present participle, but once again, this effect was only significant for the imperfect tense. Thus, it seems that writers would use the post-verbal semantic information to avoid and/or to correct pre-graphic agreement errors, but only for one tense out of two. Semantic clues were used for the verbal agreement only with the imperfect tense, and perhaps even less with the present. It is nevertheless difficult to conclude that making a verb agree with its subject requires more information for the imperfect than for the present.

As to the effect of the number of preverbal nouns, two opposed results were observed. The first confirmed Bock and Miller's (1991) and Bock and Cutting's (1992) results. For the present, agreement errors increased when the head noun was singular and the local noun plural. The second did not confirm these results in the imperfect. Thus, it appears that a plural local noun would automatically activate a plural verbal flexion and would lead writers to make more errors. However, this result was found only for the present, as in previous experiments (Chanquoy & Negro, 1996a & b; Negro & Chanquoy, 1997, submitted).

Finally, the hypothesis that predicted an interaction among the plausibility of local nouns, the nature of adverbial phrases and the number of preverbal nouns was confirmed for both tenses. The ratio of errors was the largest with a singular head noun, a plural plausible local noun, and a neutral adverb. Without any semantic information, the pre-graphic monitoring system could not detect any errors. Nevertheless, if the absence of semantic information seemed to raise agreement difficulties in the Singular-Plural condition then the increase of semantic information in sentences (a non plausible local noun plus a present participle) did not significantly decrease the ratio of errors. Therefore, we can only conclude that the absence of semantic parameters would seem to increase the syntactic ambiguity between the two competitive nouns of the preverbal phrase. These findings seem to indicate that a semantic contribution is important but not sufficient for control of noun-verb agreement.

4   GENERAL DISCUSSION

The objective of this work was to place obvious variables in sentences that could lead to or prevent subject-verb agreement errors. Until now these kinds of errors in adult expert writers were interpreted by French authors as due to a temporary over-load in working memory (Fayol & Got, 1991; Fayol, Largy & Lemaire, 1994; Largy, Chanquoy & Fayol, 1993). Conversely, for English authors working on oral language, this explanation was not acceptable (See Bock & Cutting, 1992; Bock & Miller, 1991). These authors have shown that when the length of the phrase separating the subject of the verb was manipulated, the ratio of errors did not increase. However, this increase of phrase length can be considered as raising the load in working memory and therefore, as minimizing available cognitive resources. This result relative to the phrase length has also been found in French written productions (Chanquoy & Negro, 1996b, Negro & Chanquoy, 1997). Moreover, the same experiments in the imperfect showed no effect of memory load on the ratio of agreement errors (Chanquoy & Negro, 1996a). Thus, a cognitive overload in working memory could be an explanation but it seems that it is not a sufficient explanation, at least in English oral language and in French written language, only with the imperfect tense.

The model of agreement subject-verb processing, proposed by Fayol, Largy, Hupet and Schelstraete (submitted), as well as Kellogg's model of writing (1996), have then led to formulate new hypotheses about agreement errors. According to these two models it seems that there could exist a pre-graphic monitoring process for controlling and correcting errors. In others terms, orthographic agreement errors could be detected before their graphic realization. This detection would be possible by phonological (Largy, 1995; Largy, Fayol, & Lemaire, 1996; Vigliocco, Butterworth, & Semenza, 1995) and/or semantic (Largy, 1995; Hupet, Schelstraete, Demaeght, & Fayol, 1996) information provided in sentences.

The two experiments that we have described explored some of the processing underlying number agreements of verbs in French written productions. The first experiment showed a significant effect of phonological factors, but this was restricted to the present tense. The second experiment showed an effect of semantic factors, but this was restricted to the imperfect.

It seems that French writers did not use the same information for verb agreement according to its tense. For the present tense, the useful information seems to be phonological and for the imperfect the more useful information is semantic. However, the results did not show a decrease of agreement errors with semantic or phonological information. In other words, writers did not systematically detect agreement errors when these kinds of clues were provided by the sentence. In addition, as opposed to Hupet, Schelstraete, Demaeght, and Fayol's study (1996), the agreement control was not more efficient with Plural-Singular than with Singular-Plural sentences.

Nevertheless, whatever the verbal tenses, adults made more agreement errors without any phonological or semantic information and in Singular-Plural conditions. A phonological ambiguity or a lack of semantic information associated with Singular-Plural sentences would need too many cognitive resources to allow a pre-graphic control. Conversely, when there is just one phonological ambiguity or when there are mismatched preverbal nouns, expert writers are able to control and avoid agreement errors. Thus, when writers have to deal with many ambiguities (two plausible preverbal nouns, or pseudo-plural head nouns, in Singular-Plural condition), no cognitive resources are available for controlling errors. It seems that even expert writers are not able to manage several tasks at the same time (i.e., to solve ambiguities and to activate the pre-graphic monitoring), even though these tasks are largely automatized, particularly when they exceed their limited processing resources (Richard, 1980).

One implication of these results is that the hypothesis of the existence of a pre-graphic control seems confirmed. This control seems to be cognitively costly and impossible to activate when writers have to deal with other parallel tasks. Thus, a new hypothesis dealing with pre-graphic control associated with working memory resources might explain some of our contradictory results.

Finally, in the experiment concerning semantic variables, results were different for the present and the imperfect tense. It seems that the imperfect tense is more regular than the present, and more frequent in written language. However it is difficult to conclude that the management of these two tenses could be different or could consume different cognitive resources. Much more research is needed. In addition, it would be interesting to compare the results obtained in the first experiment with those obtained in the second. The number of errors was indeed twice as frequent in the phonological than in the semantic experiment. It could be thus important to determine whether semantic clues are used or phonological ones.

To conclude, the pre-graphic or pre-phonological control, phonological and/or semantic, has been made obvious by many studies but only with adult writers and speakers. It is also important to see if children have this monitoring system available, and if they can use it. One hypothesis could be that they would not be able to use such a system because all their cognitive resources are devoted to graphic transcription and to spelling problems. For children, writing is a very complex and costly activity. Kellogg (1996) has shown that the monitoring system is very demanding on working memory. Although Kellogg's model (1996) describes adult writing, it is possible to consider that the same processes exist for children (Berninger & Swanson, 1994). These processes probably do not demand the same amount of resources for adults as for children, especially because adults have automatized some of them (for example, graphic transcription). It could thus be interesting to analyze how children manage semantic and/or phonological information while writing. This research is currently underway.

AUTHOR NOTE

The authors wish to sincerely express thanks to Sarah Ransdell for her careful and critical reading of this manuscript and for her many helpful comments.

REFERENCES

Baddeley, A.D. (1986). *Working memory*. Oxford: Clarendon Press.

Baddeley, A.D. (1990). *Human memory. Theory and practice*. Boston, London, Sydney, Toronto: Allyn & Bacon.

Baddeley, A.D., & Hitch, G. (1974). Working memory. In G.A. Bower (Ed.), *Recent advances in learning and motivation. Vol. 8* (pp. 47-90). New York: Academic Press.

Berko, J. (1958). The child's learning of English morphology. *Word, 14*, 150-177.

Berninger, V.W., & Swanson, H.L. (1994). Modification of the Hayes and Flower model to explain beginning and developing writing. In E. Butterfield (Ed.), *Advances in cognition and Educational Practice. Vol. 2: Children's writing: Toward a process theory of development of skilled writing* (pp. 57-82). Greenwich, CT: JAI Press.

Bock, K, & Cutting, J.C. (1992). Regulating energy: Performance units in language production. *Journal of Memory and Language, 31*, 99-127.

Bock, K., & Eberhard, K.M. (1993). Meaning, sound and syntax in English number agreement. *Language and Cognitive Processes, 8(1)*, 57-99.

Bock, K, & Miller, C.A. (1991). Broken agreement. *Cognitive Psychology, 23*, 45-93.

Chanquoy, L., & Negro, I. (1996a). Subject-verb agreement errors in written productions. Study in French children and adults. *Journal of Psycholinguistic Research, 25(5)*, 553-570.

Chanquoy, L., & Negro, I. (1996b). *A study of subject-verb agreement errors: A reply, in writing, of Bock and Miller (1991)*. Paper presented at the E.A.R.L.I. S.I.G. Writing Conference. University of Barcelona (Spain), October 23-25, 1996.

Fayol, M., & Got, C. (1991). Automatisme et contrôle dans la production écrite / Les erreurs d'accord sujet-verbe chez l'enfant et l'adulte. *L'Année Psychologique, 91*, 187-205.

Fayol, M., Hupet, M., Largy, P., & Schelstraete, M.A. (*submitted*). Broken agreement in written French: A two-step processing model of number agreement.

Fayol, M., Largy, P., & Lemaire, P. (1994). Cognitive overload and orthographic errors. When cognitive overload enhances subject-verb agreement errors. A study in French written language. *The Quarterly Journal of Experimental Psychology, 47A*, 437-464.

Francis, W.N. (1986). Proximity concord in English. *Journal of English Linguistics, 19*, 309-318.

Goodluck, H., & Häkansson, G. (1984). *Children's syntax - Grammar and experimental evidence*. Paper presented at the Proceedings of Child Language Symposium. Lund University. May 17-18, 1984.

Hupet, M., Fayol, M., & Schelstraete, M.A. (1998). Effects of semantic variables on the subject-verb agreement processes in writing. *British Journal of Psychology, 89*, 1-17.

Hupet, M., Schelstraete, M.A., Demaeght, N., & Fayol, M. (1996). Les erreurs d'accord sujet-verbe en production écrite. *L'Année Psychologique, 96*, 587-610.

Kellogg, R.T. (1996). A model of working memory in writing. In C.M. Levy & S. Ransdell (Eds.), *The science of writing* (pp. 57-72). Mahwah, NJ: L. Erlbaum Associates.

Largy, P. (1995). *Production et gestion des erreurs en production écrite: Le cas de l'accord sujet/verbe. Etude chez l'adulte et l'enfant*. Thèse de l'Université de Bourgogne, Dijon.

Largy, P., Chanquoy, L., & Fayol, M. (1993). Automatic and controlled writing: Subject-verb agreement errors in French native speakers. In G. Eigler, & T. Jechle (Eds), *Writing: Current trends in European research, (pp. 109-120)*. Freiburg: Hochschul Verlag.

Largy, P., Fayol, M., & Lemaire, P. (1996). The homophone effect in written French: The case of verb/noun inflection errors. *Language and Cognitive Processes, 11(3)*, 217-255.

Levelt, W.J.M. (1989). *Speaking. From intention to articulation*. Cambridge, London: M.I.T. Press.

Negro, I., & Chanquoy, L. (1995). *Charge mentale et accord sujet-verbe chez des enfants et des adultes*. Paper presented for the Workshop of the Société Française de Psychologie. Montpellier (France), July 1-2, 1995.

Negro, I., & Chanquoy, L. (1996). La charge cognitive permet-elle d'expliquer les erreurs d'accord sujet-verbe chez des adultes? *Psychologie Française, 41(4)*, 355-364.

Negro, I., & Chanquoy, L. (1997). *Mémoire de travail et production écrite: Le cas des erreurs d'accord sujet-verbe*. Paper presented for the Workshop " Working Memory and Development ", Chambéry (France), March 7-8, 1997.

Negro, I., & Chanquoy, L. (submitted). Etude d'un cas particulier de l'orthographe française: Les erreurs d'accord sujet-verbe au présent, à l'imparfait et au futur chez l'adolescent.

Negro, I., Chanquoy, L., & Fayol, M. (1994). *Effet d'une charge en mémoire sur les erreurs d'accord sujet-verbe chez des enfants (9 et 12 ans) et des adultes*. Paper presented at the Annual Conference of the Société Française de Psychologie, Montpellier (France), October 6-8, 1994.

Richard, J.F. (1980). *L'attention*. Paris: Presses Universitaires de France.

Stemberger, J.P. (1983). Inflectional malapropisms: From-based errors in English morphology. *Linguistics, 21*, 573-602.

Vigliocco, G., Butterworth, B., & Semenza, C. (1995). Constructing subject-verb agreement in speech: The role of semantic and morphological factors. *Journal of Memory and Language, 34*, 186-215.

Vygotsky, L.S. (1962). *Thought and language*. Cambridge, MA: M.I.T. Press.

Witte, S.P., & Cherry, R.D. (1994). Think-aloud protocols, protocol analysis, and research design: An exploration of the influence of writing tasks on writing processes. In P. Smagorinsky (Ed.), *Speaking about writing: Reflections on research methodology* (pp. 20-54). Thousand Oaks, CA: Sage Publications.

Writing, Reading, and Speaking Memory Spans and the Importance of Resource Flexibility

Sarah Ransdell
   Department of Psychology, Florida Atlantic University, USA
C. Michael Levy
   Department of Psychology, University of Florida, USA

ABSTRACT

Two complex working memory measures, reading span and writing span, were each found to account for significant variance in reading comprehension ability, especially for skilled readers. Speaking span, and two measures of writing span, word memory and sentence length, also predicted writing fluency and organizational quality. Resource flexibility during writing span was more successful for participants with high reading comprehension skill than low. Skilled comprehenders remembered more words when focussing on storage and wrote longer sentences when focussing on processing. Participants with low skill showed no such resource flexibility. These results support the idea that working memory aids the suppression of less advantageous strategies, especially for successful readers and writers. Complex span measures predict language skill because they are a good measure of resource flexibility in working memory.

1   INTRODUCTION

Writing well is one of the most difficult cognitive tasks. We began researching it because we noticed that skilled writers employ different strategies than less skilled writers (Levy & Ransdell, 1995; Ransdell & Levy, 1996). For example, skilled writers move rapidly and often between planning, generating text, and evaluating text. Less skilled writers view writing as a linear progression through planning what to write, typing it, and then revising only when a draft is just about finished. Skilled writers can store plans, evaluate possible new text, and type, almost concurrently. Poor writers must time share between storage and processing demands. Recently-developed models of writing include working memory as a critical component mediating the successful coordination of writing subprocesses (i.e. Hayes, 1996; Kellogg, 1996). Our research investigates the role of working memory resource flexibility as a way of explaining good writers' storage and processing skills.

Ample research has shown that skilled readers have better strategies for allocating working memory resources than those who are less skilled (Gernsbacher & Faust, 1991). For example, skilled readers can comprehend sentence meaning while simultaneously storing words and keeping track of the gist of the discourse. Poor readers cannot as easily juggle word, sentence, and story-level meaning . We report here on a measure of working memory capacity, writing span, that captures skilled readers' flexibility and should therefore predict writing success. Modeled after Daneman and Carpenter's (1980) reading span measure, it involves the storage of increasingly larger sets of words in memory while creating written sentences using the words. Reading span tests involve reading comprehension rather than writing sentences as the main processing task, but the storage tasks are the same in the two span tests. For example, in reading span, the reader reads sets containing several sentences and is asked to recall the last word in the sentences while also comprehending them. In writing span, the writer generates several sentences from sets of words given. We believe the critical element in these tasks is that they allow for a potential trade-off between storage and processing resources. One must allocate resources to both comprehending sentences (reading span) or generating them (writing span). At the same time, one must remember the end word of the sentence (reading span) or the word given (writing span). One goal of this paper is to determine whether both good readers and writers handle this trade-off better than poor readers and writers. Better writers may be able to suppress less advantageous strategies when required to do so, either generating more complex sentences or remembering more words, given the task at hand.

The extensive literature on the reading span test documents that it predicts differences in reading comprehension (Daneman & Carpenter, 1980; Daneman & Green, 1986; Daneman & Merikle, 1996; Just & Carpenter, 1992; Masson & Miller, 1983; Palmer, MacLeod, Hunt, & Davidson, 1985), fact retrieval and pronomial reference skill (Daneman & Green, 1986), the ability to draw inferences from text (Masson & Miller, 1983), lexical decision and Posner name matching times (Baddeley, Logie, Nimmo-Smith, & Brereton, 1985), syntactic processing (King & Just, 1991) and the resolution of lexical ambiguity (Miyake, Just, & Carpenter, 1994). The most common explanation for these relationships is that reading span assesses the ability to store, as well as to process, the written word in a flexible and advantageous manner.

On the other hand, simple digit or word spans generally do not predict reading comprehension because they do not require both processing and storage (Daneman & Carpenter, 1980; Masson & Miller, 1983; Perfetti & Goldman, 1976). The greater predictive power of complex spans may be a consequence of their requiring coordination of processing and storage demands. If this is true, it becomes reasonable to study the extent to which people can distribute their resources between processing and storage in reading comprehension and essay writing tasks. The next section focuses on why working memory should be particularly important for the success of organization in writing.

1.1 Working Memory and Organization in Writing

Written language production involves the simultaneous management and coordination of several writing processes, all of which require successful working memory resource flexibility (Levy & Ransdell, 1995). Previous evidence suggests that the organization of a written product in particular depends on the writer's resource flexibility among these processes. Our Six-Subgroup Quality Scale (SSQS) identifies differences in six separable components of writing quality from organization to technical quality (Ransdell & Levy, 1996). Initial research on individual differences in working memory capacity has revealed a relation between reading span and organizational quality. Madigan, Johnson, and Linton (1994) found that reading span accounted for 15% of the variance in their measure of quality. This is about half of the variance accounted for in reading comprehension by reading span (Daneman & Carpenter, 1980; Daneman & Green, 1986). Of interest here is whether the other five subgroups of quality in the SSQS (word choice, mechanics, content, purpose, and style) are similarly related to span performance. Since Madigan et al.

found reading span to be correlated with their quality measure, we predict it to be most highly correlated with our SSQS Organization subscale because in comparisons we have made, Organization is most related to Madigan's measure.

The dependence of the organization of an essay on working memory is highlighted in a study by McCutchen, Covill, Hoyne, and Mildes (1994). They found that reading span is a better predictor of writing quality when the sentences in the span task are related sets of connected discourse or a story. Story version reading span correlated .40 with quality, while the unrelated sentence reading span correlated .14. Reading spans were also higher for both skilled and less skilled students in the story version relative to when unrelated sentences were presented. In addition, more skilled writers were faster at a lexical decision task than less skilled ones. McCutchen et al. suggest that fluent translating processes (from plans in the head to words written on the page) help to reduce working memory load during reading span tests *and* during writing. We propose that not only do fluent translating processes decrease working memory load, but they are the direct result of resource flexibility differences among writers. Better writers can more easily allocate resources to sentence generation, lexical retrieval, or word memory — depending on task requirements — than can poor writers.

1.2 Working Memory and Fluency in Writing

In addition to affecting writing organization, resource flexibility may also influence writing fluency. In the realm of reading comprehension, Walczyk's compensatory-encoding model (1995) predicts that working memory resource limits will not impair readers if they are able to simply slow down. There is some evidence that writers will slow down when their working memory resources are strained. For example, Madigan, Holt and Blackwell (1993) reassigned keyboard keys to make the writing task more difficult. Under these conditions, writers with higher reading spans produced words more quickly than those with lower spans. High span writers slowed down less because the new key assignments did not slow them down as much as they did the less flexible low span writers.

One view of the advantage of a larger complex span suggests that larger units of information can be processed with a lighter load on storage capacity (Daneman & Carpenter, 1980; McCutchen et al., 1994). This enables writers to devote more resources to a multitude of writing processes. Alternatively, Walczyk (1995) proposes that compensatory strategies are employed by good readers when the task becomes increasingly difficult and that it is for this reason that they can process and store information fluently and well. Each of these contrasting views suggests that good writers will score high on complex span measures because these writers compensate for resource limits with strategic flexibility. A larger span should yield higher quality writing and greater fluency because writers can trade storage for processing and vice versa, not because processing always reduces the storage load. Hayes (1996) has proposed that individual differences in writing performance will be related to the ability to manage the often simultaneous constraints of planning, generating text, and evaluative reading. It is therefore likely that both reading and writing performance may depend on the ability to maximize working memory resource flexibility. Complex span measures have the practical and theoretical advantage of measuring such flexibility as well as predicting language production and comprehension success.

1.3 Reading and Speaking Span

Past research has focussed on whether the storage task or the processing task is more important for predicting complex performance. Some researchers suggest that what is stored is more important than what is processed (Engle, Cantor, & Carullo, 1992; Turner & Engle, 1989). For example, Engle and his colleagues report that during reading span tests, the storage task must be a word rather than a digit to predict reading ability. Others have argued that what is stored is not nearly as important as what is processed and have shown that the more similar the processing task is to the behavior being measured, the stronger the predictability (Daneman, 1987; Daneman & Tardif, 1987). For example, Daneman and Green (1986) have shown that both reading and speaking spans predict vocabulary production fluency, but that reading span no longer predicts fluency when speaking span is partialled out. We predict a similar finding for our production task, essay writing. Speaking span predicts fluency better than reading span presumably because its main processing task is production rather than comprehension. The present research extends the discussion of the relative importance of storage versus processing to the question of how storage and processing demands are coordinated in the first place. The predictive power of reading span should be higher for those with greater reading ability because good readers can more easily coordinate storage and processing than can poor readers.

Two experiments were conducted, the first looking at reading and speaking span measures as predictors of reading comprehension and writing performance, and the second, looking at an analogue of these original span measures. The purposes of Experiment 1 were to replicate the relationship between reading span, speaking span and reading comprehension, and to establish a relationship between reading and speaking spans, and writing performance. Next, in Experiment 2, three writing span measures are introduced in order to determine the impact of storage versus processing emphasis during writing on predictions of essay writing skill.

2 EXPERIMENT 1

Experiment 1 was designed to investigate the interrelationships among reading comprehension, reading span, speaking span and writing performance. We anticipated that both complex span measures will independently contribute to variance in reading and writing performance because each is a good measure of resource flexibility in working memory. Speaking span may predict writing better than reading performance because the task involves production rather than comprehension. In addition, the following new hypotheses were tested. (a) Given the findings of Madigan et al. (1993) and McCutchen et al. (1994), organization quality of an essay should be better predicted by span performance than overall quality. (b) Writing fluency should also be predicted by span performance. (c) Writing span measures should predict skilled readers' performance better than less skilled because skilled readers can flexibly allocate resources to processing or storage depending on tasks demands. Skilled readers will remember more words when asked to do so or produce longer sentences.

2.1 Method

We recruited 45 psychology students at a state university in the southeastern USA who participated for class credit. All participants were between 18 and 45 years of age (mean = 27). A writing questionnaire indicated that participants rated themselves as average in writing skill, had taken less than 10 college courses that involved writing, and wrote an average of one letter a month.

Participants were randomly divided into two groups. Half of them were first measured with two span tests, and half first wrote essays and took the comprehension test. The reading span test simultaneously draws upon the processing and storage resources of working memory during reading (Daneman & Carpenter, 1980). Participants read aloud a series of 70 unrelated sentences (adapted from Madigan, Holt, & Blackwell, 1993). Each sentence ended in a different word and was 11-16 words in length (e.g., "The engine of the car was very old even though the paint was new".). Participants were presented with 5 sets of 2, 3, 4, and 5 sentences. At the end of each set, they recalled as many of the final words in each sentence as they could. Increasingly longer sets of sentences were presented. Two measures of span were scored, the level at which complete recall of final words on 3 of 5 sets was made, and the total percentage of final words recalled. Half-credit was given if the participant was correct on 2 sets at a particular level. True/false comprehension questions were asked at random intervals at each set size to ensure that participants were reading the sentences for meaning. Reading span is typically about 3 words, with a range of 2 to 4.5 for college-level readers (Daneman & Green, 1986). Participants were not given any specific strategy to use but were simply told to remember the final word in each sentence while they read each sentence aloud for comprehension.

A speaking span test (Daneman & Green, 1986) was also administered. Here, language production rather than comprehension was the processing task. Participants were presented with increasingly larger sets of unrelated words. Each word contained 7 letters and was presented individually for one second each. At the end of the set, participants were asked to generate as many sentences as possible, each containing one of the words shown. Five sets each of 2, 3, 4, and 5 words were presented. Speaking span was defined as the largest set size where a grammatically correct sentence for each word in the set was generated correctly on 3 of 5 sets.

The other half of the 45 participants first wrote a 20-minute argumentative exposition letter on the pros and cons of lowering the state drinking age from 21 to 18 years. Participants were asked to address their letters to the Governor. Participants also took the *Nelson-Denny Reading Test (1993)*, comprehension subtest, Form G. This test contains 7 reading comprehension passages and a total of 38 test questions. Twenty minutes were allocated for the reading comprehension test. The first minute of the test was used to determine the reading rate. The standardized reading test was particularly important to determine that the general skill of the sample because these students are not required to take common achievement tests for admission.

Writing Fluency Analyses
Participants were trained in the basics of a popular word processing package. Then, a special purpose terminate and stay resident program called Keysave (Ransdell, 1990) was launched to obtain estimates of writing fluency. Participants' screens appeared normal during word processing, but each of their keystrokes and their time of occurrence was stored for later analysis. Writing fluency was defined as the number of words typed per minute during the writing session.

Writing Quality Analyses
The essays were scored using the Six-Subgroup Quality Scale (Ransdell & Levy, 1996). Each essay was rated on 13 separate dimensions of writing quality that

formed six distinct subgroups: 1) organization and development, 2) style, 3) content, 4) word choice and arrangement, 5) purpose/audience/tone, and 6) mechanics. The scale was adapted from English composition placement exams used at the University of Maine. A pair of judges rated all essays on each of the 13 dimensions one at a time on a 5-point scale. Overall inter-rater reliability was $r = .90$. The combined score of both raters on all 13 subscales was converted into a percentage and used as the overall writing quality score.

2.2 Results

The correlation between reading comprehension and reading span ($r = .46$) was reliable and identical to that found by Baddeley, Logie, Nimmo-Smith, and Brereton (1985). The relationship was somewhat lower than that obtained by Daneman and Carpenter (1980). The participants in the Baddeley et al. and the present studies were more diverse in terms of age range and educational background than those who participated in the study by Daneman and Carpenter.

Mean reading span was 3.04 words (SD = .79), comparable to those reported by Daneman and Carpenter (1983). The mean speaking span was 2.75 (SD = .64). Daneman and Green's (1986) mean was slightly higher at 3.28. Total reading and speaking span scores indicating the percentage of correct items in each span were 72% (SD = 6.6) and 67% (SD = 7), respectively. No pattern of differences existed between percentage of words recalled and level of recall in any span measure, so percents were used throughout. Reading span was similar to the value reported by Baddeley, Logie, Nimmo-Smith and Brereton (1985). The average Nelson-Denny reading comprehension score was 30.53 (SD = 4.83), which is a percentile rank of 48 for third-year college students at a 4-year university.

As hypothesized, *both* span measures contributed to the variance in reading and writing performance. The Pearson product moment correlations between reading and speaking span scores, reading comprehension, reading rate, and overall writing quality are shown in Table 1. All correlations greater than .30 were significant at an alpha level of .05. As in previous research, reading span reliably predicted reading comprehension, $r = .46$, as did speaking span, $r = .31$. Reading comprehension was also significantly correlated with overall writing quality, $r = .32$.

Multiple regression analyses were conducted to determine the relative contributions of each variable to predicting reading and writing skill. A stepwise multiple regression with reading comprehension as the criterion variable was conducted entering reading span, speaking span, and overall writing quality into a linear equation in order of relatedness. Reading span and writing quality together accounted for 30% of the variance in reading comprehension scores, ($F (2,42) = 8.33, p = .001$). Of the 30%, reading span accounted for 21% of the variance in comprehension with quality adding another 9%. Speaking span also predicted reading comprehension but the association was weaker and contributed no unique variance to reading comprehension when reading span was removed.

In hypothesis (a) we predicted that organization quality would be best predicted by span measures. In a second stepwise regression, neither span measure alone significantly predicted *overall* writing quality. Seven percent of the variance in the quality subgroup of Organization was accounted for by speaking span, $F(2,42) = 3.17, p = .03$. No other subgroup scores were reliably related to quality. Hypothesis (b) was not supported because unreliable correlations were found between span

Table 1   *Mean scores and correlations between reading and speaking span, writing quality, reading comprehension and reading rate in Experiment 1. N=45, standard deviations in parentheses.*

	Mean	Speaking span	Writing quality	Reading comp.	Reading rate
Reading span	72 (6.6)	.37*	.12	.46*	.28
Speaking span	67 (7.0)		.16	.31*	.09
Writing quality	75 (10.2)			.32*	.20
Reading comprehension	31 (4.8)				.24
Reading rate	50 (10.2)				

Note: * $p < .05$.

measures and fluency. Hypothesis (c) stated that span measures would have a higher predictive value for better readers. Reading span was significantly predictive for those who scored above the median in reading comprehension ($r = .35$) but not for those who scored below the median ($r = .24$). These two correlations were reliably different from one another, t (22) = 5.60, $p <.05$.

2.3 Discussion

Previous findings of reliable correlations among writing quality, reading and speaking span, and reading comprehension were replicated and some new multivariate relationships were discovered. Support was found for two of three new hypotheses. The quality subgroup of Organization was the only subgroup on the SSQS to be reliably related to a span measure, speaking span. And the performance of those with high reading comprehension skill were more strongly predicted by reading span than those with low skill. One hypothesis was not supported; writing fluency was not significantly correlated with the span measures. Fluency defined as simply the number of words typed per minute leaves out words created but deleted before the final draft. It was not feasible to procure this information from Keysave records. Experiment 2 included a better estimate of true fluency than was used in the first experiment by including a count of all words created *including* those deleted before the final draft.

Validation of Complex Span Measures

The best regression model for predicting reading comprehension was found to be a combination of reading span and writing quality measures. Writing quality contributes unique variance to reading comprehension over and above that of reading span. While writing is not a component process of reading, it is likely that the processes shared by reading and writing are related by resource flexibility in working memory. If one has adequate working memory resource flexibility *and* is able to create well-constructed and organized sentences, then one is also likely to read well. Furthermore, reading span is a better predictor of reading comprehension ability for those who score well on measures of reading comprehension. Our resource flexibility model suggests that because reading span assesses the ability to store as well as process the written word in a flexible and advantageous manner, then it should do better at predicting what good readers do relative to poor ones. In other words, high span indicates good agility in storing and processing information while low span indicates poor agility.

Span Predictions of Writing Quality

Speaking span accounts for no unique variance in reading comprehension ability, but correlates best with writing quality as measured by the SSQS subgroup Organization. In previous research, Organizational quality as measured by Madigan et al. (1994) also correlated with reading span. Reading span using organized rather than random sentences best predicted language skill in McCutchen et al.'s study (1994). The present study suggests that organization, rather than technical skill, word choice, content, purpose, or style, is most affected by working memory resource flexibility. While working memory certainly plays a role in lower-level processes such as retrieval from one's lexicon and store of grammatical knowledge, it also has a critical role at the higher level of organizational quality.

3   EXPERIMENT 2

Experiment 2 was designed to test the hypothesis that a writing span measure should predict writing performance at least as well as a reading or speaking span measure. And, if resource flexibility is important, good readers and writers should be more efficient in employing advantageous strategies during writing span tests. Writing span has proven to be a considerably more difficult task for our participants than other complex span measures. This difficulty caused unreliable strategy use so in Experiment 2, we imposed strategy instructions. Manipulating strategy also served to determine how flexibly participants could balance creating written sentences while storing words.

Three new writing span tests were created corresponding to three levels of storage demands: a) a Good Sentence strategy, where the focus is on sentence generation and storage is less emphasized, b) a Good Memory strategy, where the focus is on recall of words and storage is therefore emphasized and c) a Good Memory Plus span, where the focus is on recall of final sentence words in addition to the words presented and storage is most strongly emphasized. These span measures all involve sentence-level writing as the basic processing task. Given the relative difficulty and the varying resource demands of a writing span test, it should be a good measure of resource flexibility in an independent writing task. Because of time limitations and the fact that these three writing span measures are quite fatiguing, we did not also assess reading and speaking span as in Experiment 2.

Evidence that writing span predicts writing performance at least as well as reading span would suggest the importance of overall language rather than specifically reading skill resource flexibility. Skilled participants should show greater flexibility than less skilled, and writing span should better predict skilled performance than less skilled. Greater flexibility will take the form of better word memory in both Good Memory conditions and longer sentences in the Good Sentence condition. Poor writers will not be able to suppress the less advantageous strategy given task demands. Finally, we anticipate that writing fluency will correlate well with writing span because our measurement of it in Experiment 2 was more precise than it was in Experiment 1. Recall that Walcyzk's model predicts that one compensatory mechanism in the face of resource limits is slowing down; we expect our good writers to slow down less than our poor writers. Because skilled writers are likely to create many words they do not keep in their final drafts, a fluency measure that captures these extra words may be more predictive of writing quality than the measure used in Experiment 1.

3.1 Method

Sixty psychology students who had not been in Experiment 1 participated for class credit. All participants were between 20 and 45 years of age (mean = 26). A writing questionnaire indicated that participants rated themselves as average in writing skill and average in proficiency writing with word processing software. All participants had previous experience of writing using a word processor.

Experiment 2 introduced writing span tests where participants are asked to use each of three strategies in a within-subjects design. Similar to the speaking span test of Experiment 1, participants were presented 2, 3, or 4 unrelated words but now were asked to write grammatical sentences using the presented words anywhere except at the beginning or end of the sentence. The set of 5 unrelated words used in Experiment 1 spans was dropped because pilot trials indicated that few people could recall any words in a set of this size. Participants wrote the sentences on individual pieces of paper and were given 8 seconds per word in a set. Under the Good Sentence strategy, participants focused on creating the best college-level sentences possible, even at the cost of forgetting some of the words. Under the Good Memory strategy, they focused on remembering as many of the words as possible, even at the cost of producing short, dull, simple sentences. Under the Good Memory Plus strategy, the need to remember the last word of each sentence created was added to the Good Memory strategy. Cards in front of the participants reminded them of the strategy they were currently using, and all three strategies were explained and practised before the three experimental trials were given in counterbalanced order.

As in Experiment 1, participants were asked to write an argumentative exposition before taking the span tests. This time the instructions were to imagine the best possible college class in an imaginary university with unlimited funds and to write about what it would include. Scoring procedures for quality were as in Experiment 1. Participants also completed the Nelson-Denny comprehension test after the writing span tests and essay writing. Writing fluency was measured on-line as the number of words typed per minute including those created, but deleted before the final draft. This refinement to the original Keysave program made it possible to be more precise in capturing on-line revision and it probably yielded a better estimate of fluency.

3.2 Results

Table 2 shows the correlations among the measures obtained in Experiment 2 and the means and standard deviations of each. The top half summarizes the correlates of word memory in the writing span tests and the bottom half, sentence length. Each section is organized by these two predictor variables, words recalled and then sentence length for each of these criterion variables, writing quality, writing fluency, and reading comprehension.

Table 2   *Mean scores and correlations between the three writing spans (GS, GM and GMP), writing quality, reading comprehension and writing fluency in Experiment 2 for Word Memory and Sentence Length Measures. N=60, standard deviations in parentheses.*

WORD MEMORY	Mean	GM	GMP	WQ	RC	WF
Writing Span (GS)	43 (7.1)	.59*	.46*	.20	.28	.47*
Writing Span (GM)	50 (8.6)		.62*	.30*	.42*	.39*
Writing Span (GMP)	51 (7.6)			.251	.35*	.39*
Writing Quality (WQ)	74 (13.8)				.51*	.38*
Reading Comprehension (RC)	30 (5.2)					.22
Writing Fluency(WF)	18 (6.2)					

SENTENCE LENGTH	Mean	GM	GMP	WQ	RC	WF
Writing Span (GS)	7 (2.1)	.10	.12	.12	.21	-.13
Writing Span (GM)	5 (1.2)		-.24	-.38*	-.26	.08
Writing Span (GMP)	5 (.78)			-.17	-.22	.18
Writing Quality (WQ)	74 (13.8)				.51*	.38*
Reading Comprehension (RC)	30 (5.2)					.22
Writing Fluency(WF)	18 (6.2)					

Note: * p<.05

Predicting Writing Quality

A stepwise multiple regression analysis showed that *words recalled* during the Good Memory (GM) writing span accounted for unique variance (7%) in overall quality, $[F (3,54) = 4.13, p = .04]$. The essays written by participants in Experiment 2 were also scored using an essay sorting procedure devised by Johnson, Linton and Madigan (1994). The correlation between essay sort quality scores and our 13-point scale was r = .25, with inter-rater reliability averaging .65. Essay sort quality accounted for less than 1% of the variance in writing span. Our quality measures accounted for about 8% of the variance in writing span. Our overall quality scores correlated .51 with reading comprehension scores and .13 with the essay sort.

In a separate regression, *mean sentence length* accounted for 16% of the variance in quality [overall $F (3,54) = 3.44, p = .02$]. Writing span under the GM strategy alone accounted for 14% of the variance $[R = .37, F (1,56) = 9.13, p = .004]$. Under Good Sentence (GS) and GMP (Good Memory Plus) strategies, no significant unique variance accounted for quality. In sum, during writing span, both recalling more words and writing longer sentences were associated with higher quality essay writing. The Good Memory strategy for both writing span measures was most predictive of quality. Writing span can predict writing quality at least as well as reading span.

Predicting Writing Fluency

Writing fluency was also significantly related to *words recalled* in writing span $[R = .45,$ overall $F (3,45) = 3.74, p = .01]$. In an univariate analysis, words recalled when under GS strategies accounted for 17% of the variation in fluency $[R = .41, F (1,47) = 9.67, p = .003]$. Span under GM or GMP strategies added nothing significant to the regression. Writing fluency was significantly correlated with writing quality $[R = .39, F (3,43) = 2.60, p = .05]$. An univariate regression showed that pause duration (the average number of seconds between pauses rather than words per minute) accounted for 15% of the variance in quality scores but words per minute did not add any unique predictive power, $[F (1,46) = 8.34, p = .006]$. In sum, fluency can be predicted by words recalled in writing span, but not by sentence length in writing span.

Predicting Reading Comprehension
Words recalled during writing span under GM and GMP strategies predicted reading comprehension $(R = .32)$ as well as speaking span did in Experiment 1. In a stepwise multiple regression with reading comprehension as the criterion variable, mean number of words recalled under GM and GMP writing span, accounted for a significant 10% of the variance in reading comprehension scores $[F (2,57) = 6.59, p = .01]$. Under the GS strategy, writing span did not uniquely contribute to variance in reading comprehension. *Mean sentence length*, on the other hand, did not significantly predict reading comprehension under the GS strategy, $(R = .21)$ nor under GM and GMP strategies, $Rs = -.26$ and $-.25$, respectively. A multiple regression analysis indicated that sentence length under the GS strategy contributed 6% of the variance in reading comprehension and GM and GMP another 6%, $[F (2,57) = 3.80, p = .02]$.

As in Experiment 1, writing quality was significantly correlated with reading comprehension $(r = .50)$. This correlation is similar to that of Breland and Jones' (1984) comparison of verbal SAT as a measure of reading comprehension and writing quality $(r = .56)$.

Writing Span Predicts High Reading Comprehension Skill
Two separate multiple regression analyses were conducted on participants high and low on Nelson-Denny reading comprehension test using a median split. Those participants above the median in comprehension skill had 29% of the variance in comprehension scores accounted for by word memory in the writing span tests $[R = .54, F (3,28) = 3.86, p = .02]$. Those participants low in comprehension skill did not account for significant variance in comprehension by writing span, $[F (3,24) = 1.84, p = .16]$. Pairwise comparison tests using t with Bonferroni adjustment showed that those with high reading comprehension were able to remember significantly more words under the GM strategy than the GS, $t (31) = 4.31, p = .001$. They also remembered more words under the GMP than the GS, $t (31) = 3.36, p = .02$. GMP and GM strategies were not significantly different from one another. The lack of a correlation between span and comprehension among those scoring below the median was not due to a restricted range because the standard deviation was 2.4, not significantly different to that of those scoring above the median in reading comprehension (SD = 2.8), Fmax = 1.16, $p > .05$. In sum, resource flexibility is important for correlations between span, writing and reading. Span predicts the performance of better writers and readers, but not poorer.

Writing Span Performance
The total percentage of words recalled in the writing span tests was, on average, 48% (Good Sentence = 43%, SD = 7.1, Good Memory = 50%, SD = 8.6, and Good Memory Plus = 51%, SD = 7.6). In a pilot study, test-retest reliability for each span test was, on average, .56. Strategy manipulations were successful. Memory performance was better during GM and GMP conditions than during the GS condition as revealed by using Bonferroni's adjustment (GM vs. GS, $t (59) = 3.38, p = .01$; GMP

versus GS, t (59) = 3.69, p = .001) but there was no difference between the two memory strategies (GM versus GMP, t (59) = .43). Sentences were longer during the GS condition than during the GM condition, t (59) = 7.48, or GMP condition, t (59) = 8.15. GM and GMP did not differ in sentence length, t < 1. The mean length of sentences created in each condition was overall 5.6 words per sentence (GS = 7.2; GM = 4.9; and GMP = 4.9).

Performance during writing span measures (48%) was not as successful as during the reading and speaking span measures in Experiments 2 and 1 (72% and 67%, respectively). The mean Nelson-Denny reading comprehension score was comparable to that of Experiment 1, (30.25, SD = 5.2, percentile rank = 48) indicating that Experiment 2 participants were sampled from the same population. Overall quality was slightly higher in Experiment 2 (mean of 74%, SD = 13.8) than in Experiment 1 (mean of 68%). In all analyses, there were no significant effects for writing span condition order.

4 DISCUSSION

Writing span predicted writing performance for both quality (word memory, 7% of the variance in quality; sentence length, 16% of the variance) and fluency measures when all words created were included in the analysis (word memory, 17% of the variance). Reading span was comparably predictive of quality as well in Johnson, Linton and Madigan (1994). Writing span also predicted reading comprehension performance (word memory, 10% of the variance; sentence length, 6%). Furthermore, word memory in writing span accounted for 29% of the variance in skilled comprehenders' performance, but no significant variance in less skilled. Although our results are preliminary given the newness of the writing span measure, our resource flexibility model explains these relationships by defining writing span as a good measure of resource flexibility. Perhaps most important for our model, skilled participants wrote longer sentences and remembered more words when the task demanded each strategy. Poor participants were not able to suppress less advantageous strategies; they remembered as many words in the Good Sentence condition as in the Good Memory, and wrote as long a sentence in the Good Memory as in the Good Sentence.

Writing span scores on the whole were only about two-thirds as high as the reading or speaking span performance of Experiment 1. As a consequence, initial measures of writing span reliability were low until the two strategy conditions of Experiment 2 were imposed. It was serendipitous that writing span was sufficiently difficult to require two strategy conditions because the two tasks represent a tradeoff. The more words generated per sentence, the more difficult it is to simultaneously remember words presented. This situation allowed us to discover that participants with high reading comprehension skill were able to remember more words under the good memory instructions and write longer sentences under the good sentence instructions. Higher reading comprehension ability afforded greater general processing flexibility than lower, even on a task involving writing as the main task. Previous research by Gernsbacher and Faust (1991) showed that less skilled comprehenders have less efficient suppression mechanisms than more skilled. In the present experiment, participants with high reading comprehension skill may have been able to suppress the strategy that was less advantageous in each writing span test. Support for this interpretation comes from Walczyk's (1995) finding that under pressure, skilled readers' performance is better predicted by verbal memory span than when not under pressure.

5 CONCLUSIONS

The goals of this research were to determine the type of working memory measures that predict individual differences in writing performance and to find support for a resource flexibility explanation of this predictability. Reading comprehension is clearly related to the ability to create well-organized text fluently. Both reading and writing skill are mediated by working memory flexibility, especially for skilled readers and writers. This strategic flexibility is likely to be a general system because writing span predicts reading comprehension ability as well as it does writing performance. At least within the language domain, this general capacity will vary as a function of how efficient an individual is at the specific demands of the task to which working memory is applied (see also Daneman, 1990). It might be argued that complex spans simply predict the same processes that they themselves include; reading span predicts reading, and writing span predicts writing. However, our results show that reading span can also predict writing, and writing span can predict reading. Outside the language domain, Daneman and Merikle's (1996) meta-analysis of reading span relationships shows that an individual's efficiency at executing a wide range of symbolic manipulations is related to reading comprehension. For example, Turner and Engle's (1989) math span also predicts reading comprehension, especially when the storage task is verbal (e.g., remembering a word) and when the process task is a mathematical computation.

Our results provide preliminary support for a resource flexibility explanation of working memory contributions to reading and writing skill. While the generality of working memory in nonlanguage domains is beyond the scope of this paper, these results suggest that linkages between language skills and memory are most clear when both domain specificity and strategy selection are considered. The results also suggest that the critical component of span measures is the trade-off between storage and processing rather than either demand alone. Language skills require shared working memory capacity, but differ in resource allocation priorities given to the demands of remembering, reading, and writing. In particular, writing requires resource flexibility in order for the writer to successfully attend to higher level demands such as, organization of sentences, paragraphs, and entire essays. In contrast, attending to lower-level details, such as spelling, grammar, and punctuation, are less dependent on individual differences in resource flexibility.

AUTHOR NOTE

We would like to thank Joachim Grabowski and Ron Kellogg for helpful comments on earlier versions of this chapter. We also thank Debbie Bristol, Laura Iovino, and Denise Wood for help in data collection, and Jessica Feola, Ken Galup, Lewis Orrell, Jim Roberts, and Karen Windhorst for help with data analysis. Portions of this paper were presented at the 8th Annual Computers and Writing Conference, London, UK, September 1995, and the 35th annual Psychonomics Society conference in St. Louis MO, November 1994. Correspondence should be addressed to the first author at 2912 College Avenue, Florida Atlantic University, Ft. Lauderdale, FL 33314 or RANSDELL@FAU.EDU

REFERENCES

Baddeley, A. D., Logie, R., Nimmo-Smith, I., & Brereton, N. (1985). Components of fluent reading. *Journal of Memory and Language, 24*, 119-131.

Breland, H. M., & Jones, R. J. (1984). Perception of writing skills. *Written Communication, 1*, 101-119.

Daneman, M. (1987). Reading and working memory. In J. R. Beech & A. M. Colley, (Eds.) *Cognitive approaches to reading*. NY: Wiley & Sons.

Daneman, M. (1990). Working memory as a predictor of verbal fluency. *Journal of Psycholinguistic Research, 20*, 445-464.

Daneman, M., & Carpenter, P. A. (1980). Individual differences in working memory and reading. *Journal of Verbal Learning and Verbal Behavior, 19*, 450-466.

Daneman, M., & Carpenter, P. A. (1983). Individual differences in integrating information between and within sentences. *Journal of Experimental Psychology, 9*, 561-584.

Daneman, M., & Green, I. (1986). Individual differences in comprehending and producing words in context. *Journal of Memory and Language, 25*, 1-18.

Daneman, M., & Merikle, P. M. (1996). Working memory and language comprehension: A meta-analysis. *Psychonomic Bulletin and Review, 3*, 422-433.

Daneman, M., & Tardif, T. (1987). Working memory and reading skill re-examined. In M. Coltheart (Ed.) *Attention and performance XII*, London: Erlbaum.

Engle, R. W., Cantor, J., & Carullo, J. J. (1992). Individual differences in working memory and comprehension: a test of four hypotheses. *Journal of Experimental Psychology: Learning, Memory and Cognition, 18*, no. 5, 972-992.

Gernsbacher, M. A., & Faust, M. E. (1991). The mechanism of suppression: A component of general comprehension skill. *Journal of Experimental Psychology: Learning, Memory and Cognition, 17*, 245-262.

Hayes, J. R. (1996). A new model of cognition and affect in writing. In C. M. Levy & S.E. Ransdell (Eds.) *The science of writing* (pp. 1-27). Mahwah, NJ: Lawrence Erlbaum Associates .

Jeffery, G. C. (1996). The relationship between writing span and writing skill. Paper presented at the *European Conference on Computers and Writing*, Barcelona, Spain.

Johnson, S., Linton, P., & Madigan, R. (1994). The role of internal standards in discourse. *Discourse Processes, 18*, 231-245.

Kellogg, R. T. (1996). A model of working memory in writing. In C. M. Levy & S.E. Ransdell (Eds.) *The science of writing* (pp. 57-71). Mahwah, NJ: Lawrence Erlbaum Associates.

King, J. & Just, M. A. (1991). Individual differences in syntactic processing: the role of working memory, *Journal of Memory and Language, 30*, 580-602.

Levy, C. M., & Ransdell, S. E. (1995). Is writing as difficult as it seems? *Memory and Cognition, 23*, 767-779.

Madigan, R. J., Holt, J., & Blackwell, J. (1993). The role of working memory in writing fluently. Paper presented at the 34th annual meeting of the Psychonomics Society in Washington, D. C.

Madigan, R. J., Johnson, S. E., & Linton, P. W. (1994). Working memory capacity and the writing process. Paper presented at the American Psychological Society in Washington, D. C.

Masson, M. E., & Miller, J. A. (1983). Working memory and individual differences in comprehension and memory of text. *Journal of Educational Psychology, 75*, 314-318.

McCutchen, D., Covill, A., Hoyne, S., & Mildes, K. (1994). Individual differences in writing: Implications of translating fluency. *Journal of Educational Psychology, 86*, 256-266.

Miyake, A., Just, M. A., & Carpenter, P. A. (1994). Working memory constraints on the resolution of lexical ambiguity: Maintaining multiple interpretations in neutral contexts. *Journal of Memory and Language, 33*, 175-202.

Nelson, M. S., & Denny, E. D. (1993). *The Nelson-Denny Reading Test*. Boston: Houghton-Mifflin.

Palmer, J., MacLeod, C. M., Hunt, E., & Davidson, J. E. (1985). Information processing correlates of reading. *Journal of Memory and Language, 24*, 59-88.

Perfetti, C. A., & Goldman, S. R. (1976). Discourse memory and reading comprehension skill. *Journal of Verbal Learning and Verbal Behavior, 14*, 33-42.

Ransdell, S. E. (1990). Using a real-time replay of students' word processing to understand and promote better writing. *Behavior Research Methods, Instruments, and Computers, 22*, 142-144.

Ransdell, S. E., & Levy, C. M. (1996). Working memory constraints on writing performance. In C. M. Levy & S. E. Ransdell (Eds.) *The science of writing* (pp.93-101). Mahwah, NJ: Lawrence Erlbaum Associates.

Turner, M. L. & Engle, R. W. (1989). Is working memory capacity task dependent? *Journal of Memory and Language, 28,* 127-154.

Walczyk, J. J. (1995). Testing a compensatory-encoding model. *Reading Research Quarterly, 30,* 396-408.